MADEIRA

CHRISTOPHER CATLING

DK

EYEWITNESS TRAVEL

Left **Funchal Casino** Middle **Flower sellers at Funchal market** Right **Casks of Verdelho Madeira**

DK

LONDON, NEW YORK,
MELBOURNE, MUNICH AND DELHI
www.dk.com

Produced by DP Services,
31 Ceylon Road, London W14 0PY

Printed and bound in China

First published in the UK in 2005 by Dorling Kindersley Limited
80 Strand, London WC2R 0RL
A Penguin Random House Company

15 16 17 18 10 9 8 7 6 5 4 3 2 1

Reprinted with revisions 2007, 2009, 2011, 2013, 2015

 A CIP catalogue record is available from the British Library.

ISBN 978-0-24100-788-4

Within each Top 10 list in this book, no hierarchy of quality or popularity is implied. All 10 are, in the editor's opinion, of roughly equal merit.

FSC www.fsc.org MIX Paper from responsible sources FSC™ C018179

Contents

Madeira's Top 10

The information in this DK Eyewitness Top 10 Travel Guide is checked regularly.
Every effort has been made to ensure that this book is as up-to-date as possible at the time of going to press. Some details, however, such as telephone numbers, opening hours, prices, gallery hanging arrangements and travel information are liable to change. The publishers cannot accept responsibility for any consequences arising from the use of this book, nor for any material on third party websites, and cannot guarantee that any website address in this book will be a suitable source of travel information. We value the views and suggestions of our readers very highly. Please write to: Publisher, DK Eyewitness Travel Guides, Dorling Kindersley, 80 Strand, London, WC2R 0RL, UK, or email: travelguides@dk.com.

Cover: Front – **4Corners:** Günter Gräfenhain main. **Alamy Images:** Robert Harding Picture Library Ltd/H P Merten bl. Spine: **DK Images:** Rough Guides/Helena Smith b. Back: **DK Images:** Rough Guides/Helena Smith tr; Linda Whitwam tc,tl.

Left **Ribeira da Janela islets** Middle **Capela dos Milagres, Machico** Right **The beach, Porto Santo**

Left **View from Bica de Cana** Right **Ponta de São Lourenço**

MADEIRA'S TOP 10

TOP 10 Madeira Highlights

Madeira is an island of astonishing contrasts. From the big-city sophistication of the capital, Funchal, it is a short step to the primeval woodland that cloaks the dramatic cliffs and canyons of the island's interior. The fertility of Madeira's flower-filled gardens is in marked contrast to the aridity of the island's volcanic peaks. And nothing could be more different than the gentle rippling of the levadas (canals), which carry water into Madeira's deepest valleys, and the crash of the waves that dash the island's rocky shores. Madeira has been called a place where all the continents meet. It has something of them all – including snow.

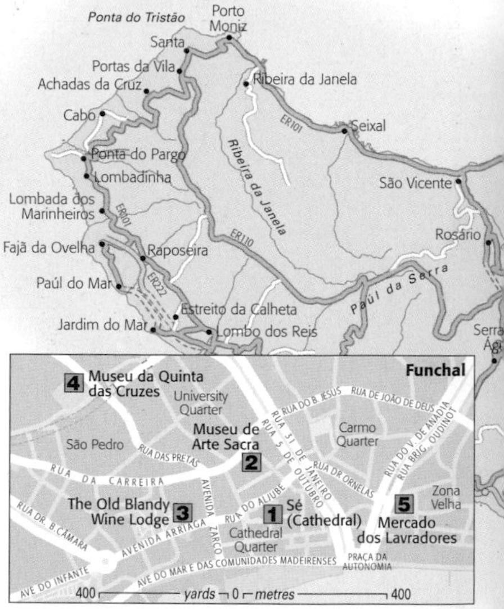

1 Funchal Cathedral (Sé)

Hewn out of the island's volcanic rock and its abundant timber supplies, Madeira's cathedral is a monument to the faith and piety of the island's first settlers *(see pp8–9)*.

2 Museu de Arte Sacra, Funchal

Trade contacts with Antwerp in the 15th century enabled Madeira's merchants to sell their sugar – so valuable that it was known as "white gold" – and buy the superb Flemish paintings and sculptures that fill this art museum *(see pp10–11)*.

3 The Old Blandy Wine Lodge, Funchal

Madeira is renowned for its wines, famous for their complexity and depth of flavour. At this historic wine lodge you can learn to be a Madeira connoisseur *(see pp12–13)*.

4 Museu da Quinta das Cruzes, Funchal

Look inside a gracious Madeiran mansion, built on the site where the island's first ruler, João Gonçalves Zarco, had his home *(see pp14–17)*.

Preceding pages **View of Curral das Freiras, with Pride of Madeira flowers in foreground**

Jardim Botânico, Funchal 6

The Botanical Gardens are a showcase for all the plants that thrive in the island's warm and humid climate, from jungle orchids to bristling cacti *(see pp20–23)*.

5 Mercado dos Lavradores, Funchal

The Farmers' Market is a bustling medley of colourful stalls positively bursting with exotic fruits, scented flowers and examples of local crafts *(see pp18–19)*.

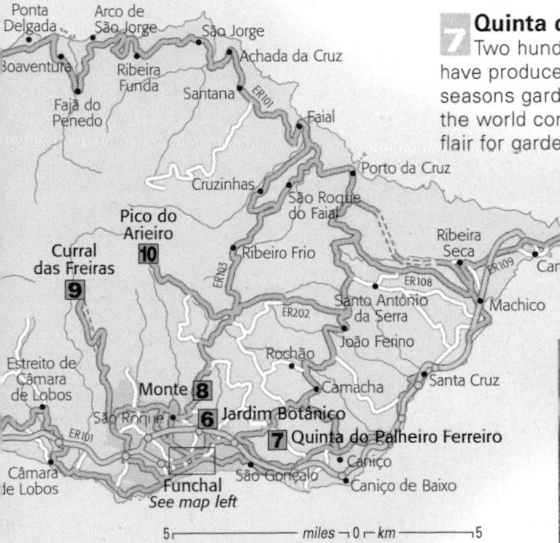

7 Quinta do Palheiro Ferreiro

Two hundred years of cultivation have produced this magnificent all-seasons garden where the flowers of the world combine with the English flair for garden design *(see pp24–5)*.

8 Monte

Escape to a romantic world of gardens, tea-houses and cobbled walks, home to Emperor Charles I in exile. Afterwards, return to the capital on the exhilarating Monte toboggan run *(see pp26–7)*.

9 Curral das Freiras

During pirate attacks, the nuns of Santa Clara took refuge in this hidden green valley encircled by sheer cliffs – a place of breathtaking scenic beauty *(see pp30–31)*.

10 Pico do Arieiro

Feel on top of the world as you view the ridges and ravines of the island's mountainous interior from the summit of Madeira's third highest peak (1,818 m; 5,965 ft) *(see pp32–3)*.

TOP 10 Funchal Cathedral (Sé)

Save for a flurry of pinnacles at the eastern end, Funchal Cathedral's exterior is very plain. By contrast, the interior is lined with statues, paintings and gold-covered chapels; the ceiling is of spectacular knotwork inspired by Moorish geometry; and set in the floor are the tombs of early bishops and sugar merchants. Designed by Pêro Anes, assisted by master mason Gil Enes, the cathedral was begun in 1493. Consecrated in September 1514, when Funchal was officially granted city status, it was finally completed in October 1517.

Funchal Cathedral

The cathedral marks the social heart of Funchal. The pavement cafés to the south (the Café Funchal and the Café Apolo) are popular meeting places for people who live and work in the city centre, and great places to relax and simply watch the world go by.

The cathedral is a functioning religious building, and visits are not encouraged during services (weekdays at 8am, 8.30am, 11.15am and 6pm; Sundays at 8am, 9am, 11am, 5pm and 6:15pm). If you go to a service, you will be able to see the normally dark interior of the church lit up.

- *Largo da Sé*
- *Map P3*
- *Open 9am–noon, 4–6pm daily*
- *Free*

Top 10 Features

1. West Portal
2. Narthex and Baptistry
3. Nave and South Aisle
4. North Aisle
5. Ceiling
6. South Transept
7. Sanctuary
8. Seating in the Sanctuary
9. Altarpiece
10. East End

1 West Portal

King Manuel I of Portugal (1495–1521) helped to fund the construction of the cathedral, and it is his coat of arms *(above)* over the Gothic doorway. The rose window above the crown is carved from rust-red local basalt.

2 Narthex and Baptistry

The vestibule to the church is paved in worn, 16th-century tomb slabs of black basalt. A wall plaque *(right)* records the visit of Pope John Paul II on 12 May 1991. To the left is the massive 16th-century font of the Gothic baptistry.

3 Nave and South Aisle

Here, floor memorials to bishops and merchants carved in marble and basalt reflect the 16th-century Portuguese style.

The Portuguese word for cathedral is Sé, which means "seat", a reference to the bishop's throne, the symbol of his authority.

4 North Aisle

Madeira's trade links with Antwerp are reflected in an unusual 16th-century brass Flemish-style memorial set in the floor to the west of the first chapel. The brass depicts the fashionable merchant Pedro de Brito Oliveira Pestana and his wife Catarina.

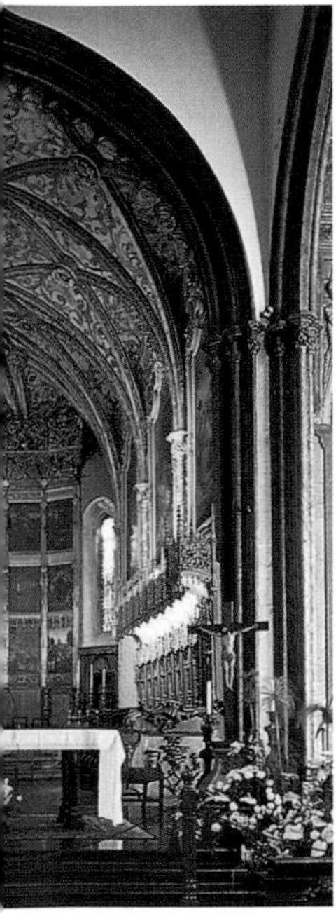

5 Ceiling

Madeira's native white cedar trees were used to brilliant effect in the construction of the ceiling of the nave, aisles and transepts *(above)*. It is one of the finest examples in Portugal of the *alfarge*, or "knotwork", technique, which blends Moorish and European elements.

6 South Transept

Sunlight floods through the transept windows to light up the timber ceiling with its everlasting knots forming arabesques and stars. Faded figures around the edge of the ceiling depict Fortune holding a billowing sail, centaurs and fish-tailed mermen.

7 Sanctuary

The nautical theme continues on the gilded ceiling of the sanctuary *(right)*, where a carving of an armillary sphere (a navigation aid) can be seen among the painted cherubs and floral swags.

8 Seating in the Sanctuary

Carved in 1510–11, and attributed to Flemish sculptor Olivier de Gand, the bold blue-and-gold choir stalls depict saints, the Apostles and prophets dressed in the elaborate attire of merchants.

9 Altarpiece

The huge altarpiece *(above)* was made in the early 16th century. Set within its ornate Gothic frames are 12 scenes from the lives of Christ and the Virgin.

10 East End

Go outside to the east end for the best view of the spire, and for the bravado display of barley-sugar pinnacles and pierced balustrades.

Knotwork Ceilings

Funchal cathedral has one of the richest and most elaborate of Portuguese knotwork ceilings, comparable in splendour to the ceiling of the Chapel of the Royal Palace at Sintra. Funchal's delirious and dizzying pattern of knots and lozenges, with projections similar to stalactites, is based on the rich geometric art of medieval Islam. Much of Portugal was under Moorish rule from AD 711 to AD 1249, and the Moors also ruled over Andalusia in Spain until 1492, precisely one year before work started on this cathedral.

Bring binoculars if you want to see the finer details of the ceiling and altarpiece. Allow time for your eyes to adjust to the gloom.

TOP 10 Museu de Arte Sacra, Funchal

Madeira is not the first place you would think to look for some of the finest Flemish masterpieces ever painted, but the 15th-century sugar trade between Funchal and Antwerp (in modern Belgium) provides the link. Merchants and plantation owners sought immortality by commissioning altarpieces for their local churches, often depicting themselves and their families kneeling in prayer. Thus the gorgeously colourful paintings gathered in this museum of religious art serve also as portraits of some of the island's first settlers.

Entrance Hall

The Renaissance *loggia* facing onto Praça do Município has been converted into the chic Café do Museu. A great place for a snack, lunch or early evening meal, the café serves salads, pasta dishes, soups and light meals from 10am to 7:30pm.

- *Rua do Bispo 21*
- *Map P3*
- *291 228 900*
- *www.museuartesacrafunchal.org*
- *Open 10am–12:30pm & 2:30–6pm Tue–Sat, 10am–1pm Sun*
- *Admission €3*

Top 10 Features

1. Entrance Hall
2. Processional Cross
3. St Sebastian
4. The *Last Supper* Tableau
5. *St James* by Dieric Bouts
6. *Deposition* by Gerard David
7. *Annunciation* by Joost van Cleve
8. *St Philip and St James* by van Aelst
9. *St Anne and St Joachim*
10. The Machico *Adoration*

1 Entrance Hall

The importance of the bishop in local society is reflected in the elegance of his palace, which now houses the museum. Visitors enter through a handsome hall floored with pebbles forming swags and garlands. The Baroque stone staircase, dating from the 1750s, is flanked by gilded candelabra.

2 Processional Cross

This exquisite example of the silversmith's art was donated at the dedication of Funchal's cathedral in 1514 by King Manuel I of Portugal (1495–1521). Tier upon tier of Gothic niches are filled with tiny figures of saints, as well as dramatic scenes from the Passion and Crucifixion of Christ.

3 St Sebastian

This early 16th-century painted stone statue, carved by Diogo Pires, is full of holes that once held arrows. St Sebastian, the Roman martyr, was condemned to death for his faith. He miraculously survived the arrows, but was later beheaded.

4 The *Last Supper* Tableau

This almost life-size tableau in painted wood was carved for the cathedral in 1648 by Manuel Pereira. Judas, who will betray Christ, sits alone clutching a money bag.

For works of religious art still in their original setting **See pp40–41**

5 *St James* by Dieric Bouts

This study of St James was probably painted in Bruges in the 1470s. The saint's gorgeous scarlet cloak and the flower-filled meadow in which he stands are typical of Flemish master Dieric Bouts' love of colour and naturalistic detail.

6 *Deposition* by Gerard David

The Virgin's face shows sadness and resignation as her Son is taken down from the Cross in the central panel of this triptych of 1518. The side panels depict the donors – Simon Acciaiuoli, a merchant from Florence (with St Bernardino of Siena), and his wife Maria (with St James).

7 *Annunciation* by Joost van Cleve

The fruits of Europe's expanding trade connections can be seen in this serene painting of around 1515 *(above)*: Mary's feet rest on an oriental carpet, and the lilies symbolizing her purity are standing in a Delft jar.

8 *St Philip and St James* by Pieter Coecke van Aelst

Here *(above)*, the donors, pictured kneeling on either side of the central panel, have been identified as Simão Gonçalves de Câmara, grandson of Zarco, and his wife Isabel.

9 *St Anne and St Joachim*

This fascinating early 16th-century painting of the Antwerp School *(right)* is reputed to show King Ladislaw III of Poland *(see p37)* and his wife Senhorina Eanes. Known as Henry the German, the king gave up his crown and became a farmer on Madeira in 1454.

10 The Machico *Adoration*

Rich in detail, this anonymous painting of around 1518 from the church at Machico *(see p87)* depicts Madeiran merchants and landowners in the guise of the Three Kings, with their servants.

Flemish Art

Madeiran art patrons would probably not have visited Antwerp or Bruges to sit for their portraits. Instead, they might have sent a sketch (perhaps drawn by one of the island's architects or masons) or perhaps relied on a friend to give the artist an accurate verbal description. In any case, exact likeness was not the artist's aim. Following the Mannerist tendency, the painter of the Machico *Adoration* emphasizes distinctive facial features – a large nose or a double chin – in order to give greater character to his subjects.

TOP 10 The Old Blandy Wine Lodge, Funchal

Plenty of places on Madeira offer wine tastings, but none will give you such a solid introduction to the history of its unique wine. With its heavy ancient beams and its cobblestone courtyards, the Old Blandy Wine Lodge feels as old as time. It is set in the surviving parts of a 17th-century Franciscan friary, most of which was demolished when Portugal passed its laws banning religious orders in 1834. The premises were acquired by the Blandy family (see p25) *in 1840 and have been used ever since for making Madeira wine.*

Sampling Madeira wine at the Max Romer Tasting Bar

To the west of the wine lodge, there is an outdoor café in the cloister of the São Francisco friary, now a delightful public garden.

You can wander in and out of the wine lodge whenever it is open. Wines may be sampled in the Max Romer Tasting Bar, and all wines, including vintages, are payable by the glass. The cost is refundable when a bottle of wine is purchased, except for vintage and package tours.

- *Avenida Arriaga 28*
- *Map P3*
- *291 228 978*
- *www.blandywinelodge.com*
- *Open 10am–6:30pm Mon–Fri, 10am–1pm Sat*
- *Admission free*
- *Tours: 10:30am, 2:30pm, 3:30pm & 4:30pm Mon–Fri, 11am Sat.*
- *Lodge Tour: €3.30, Premium Tour: €5.50, Vintage Tour: €13*

Top 10 Features

1. Courtyard
2. 18th-century Wine Press
3. Goatskins
4. Attics
5. Wine Shop
6. Wine Museum
7. Max Romer Tasting Bar
8. Vintage Room
9. Shopping Arcade
10. The "Oldest Street"

1 Courtyard

The romantic inner courtyard of the wine lodge is shaded by some of the island's tallest banana trees *(above)*. It is ringed by three storeys of attics with wisteria-draped external balconies supported on massive timber brackets.

2 18th-century Wine Press

A traditional 18th-century wine press carved with the Jesuit symbol of a cross within a triangle is on display in the courtyard. The Jesuits ran the island's wine trade until the late 18th century. English and Scottish merchants then took it over.

3 Goatskins

Wine made all over the island was brought for sale to Funchal. Porters called *borracheiros* sipped from the 40-litre loads of wine that they carried in goatskins.

4 Attics

Massive timbers support three storeys of ventilated attics *(below)*. Wines here are aged in casks warmed only by the sun, a method known as "Canteiro" that produces quality wines.

For more on Madeira wines **See pp58–9**

5 Wine Shop

This contemporary shop stocks a large selection of wines by producers from the Madeira Wine Company; as well as spirits, Madeiran liqueurs and Portuguese table wines. Connoisseurs will enjoy browsing the wine paraphernalia.

6 Wine Museum

Framed letters of appreciation from kings and queens, emperors, presidents and prime ministers – all of them lovers of good Madeira wine – line the walls of the museum at the heart of the lodge. Also on display here are leather-bound ledgers recording every sale going as far back as the 18th century.

7 Max Romer Tasting Bar

The delightfully sunny murals of grape-growing and harvesting that cover the walls of the tasting bar on the ground floor were painted in 1922 by the German artist Max Romer (1878–1960).

8 Vintage Room

Within the Vintage Room, precious wines are stored by date and kept locked behind bars. Madeira wines dating back to the early 20th century can be sampled here. Those who cannot afford the above can try moderately priced, but nevertheless appealing, 1980s vintages.

9 Shopping Arcade

In a sign of the times, the old cooper's yard has been converted into a shopping arcade. However, the Madeira Wine Company still employs coopers to patch and mend 100-year-old barrels. The coopers use traditional methods, mixing new and old oak.

10 The "Oldest Street"

The street that runs up the eastern side of the wine lodge dates from the 1400s. In the early days of Madeira's settlement, wine barrels were once dragged across the cobbles on a sledge going to and from the harbour.

Madeira Wine

Madeira wine has two defining characteristics. First, like sherry and port, it is "fortified" by the addition of brandy at the end of the fermentation process. Second, it is heated during production. The benefits of heating were discovered when wines left on board ship after a round trip to the equator were found to have developed a new depth and complexity of flavour. In time, winemakers worked out how to recreate the effect by maturing the wine in lofts heated by the sun, without the need for a sea journey. *(See also p59 on* estufagem.)

Madeira's wine industry was nearly wiped out when the vines were attacked by mildew in 1852, and by phylloxera (vine louse) in 1872.

Top 10 Museu da Quinta das Cruzes, Funchal

Madeira's early settlers built their homes on the heights above the harbour so that they could see pirate ships approaching. The Quinta das Cruzes is just such an estate. Originally built by Captain Zarco (see p36), *it was later rebuilt as the elegant home of the Lomelino family, and is now a museum full of decorative artwork. An excursion to the Quinta can be combined with a visit to the Convento de Santa Clara* (see pp16–17), *a short walk away.*

Museu da Quinta das Cruzes

There's a delightful teahouse in the gardens of the museum, with a view over Funchal's bay.

Concerts are often held in the Museu da Quinta das Cruzes; look out for posters in the ticket office.

It's a steep climb to the museum but you can take the bus marked Route Eco at any stop in the centre of Funchal, or take a taxi.

- *Calçada do Pico 1*
- *Map N2*
- *291 740 670*
- *www.museuquintadascruzes.com*
- *10am–12:30pm & 2–5:30pm Tue–Sun*
- *Admission €3*

Top 10 Features

1. Archaeological Park
2. Manueline Windows
3. Orchid Garden
4. Chapel
5. Exhibitions
6. Drawing Rooms
7. *Picnic* by Tomás da Anunciação
8. Palanquin
9. Sugar Box Furniture
10. Silver Collection

1 Archaeological Park

The gardens to the south of the Quinta *(above)* serve as an outdoor museum of archaeological remains. One prominent piece is a fragment of Funchal's pillory, erected in 1486. Until 1835, criminals were chained to the pillory and whipped.

2 Manueline Windows

The stone window frames set up in the garden *(right)* are fine examples of a style inspired by the voyages of discovery made during the reign of King Manuel I of Portugal (1495–1521). They are carved with knotted ships' ropes, leaves and other assorted flora, plus a series of lions.

3 Orchid Garden

A stately old dragon tree *(see p21)* thrusts its fleshy limbs through the roof of the shade house at the rear of the Quinta garden, where tier upon tier of tropical orchids are grown for use as cut flowers.

4 Chapel

The chapel, dating from 1692, contains the tomb of Urbano Lomelino *(above)*, an early sugar merchant who migrated to the island from Italy in the early 1500s.

5 Exhibitions

The museum hosts a permanent exhibition of decorative arts from the 15th–19th century, which encompasses paintings, sculpture, ceramics, jewellery and furniture, including a display of 19th-century drawings and watercolours of Madeira.

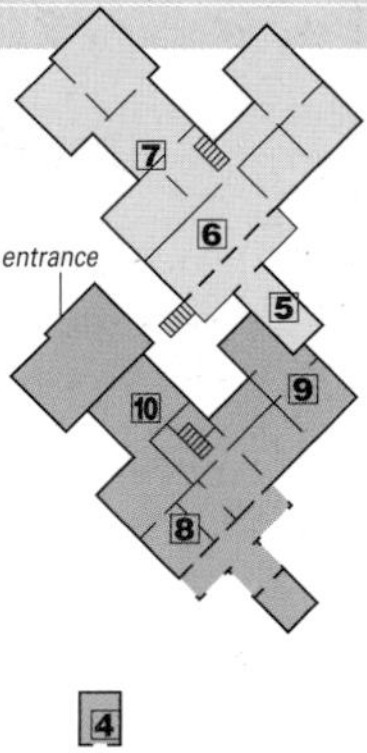

Key

- Ground Floor
- First Floor

6 Drawing Rooms

Zarco's original mansion was a busy working farm and administrative centre, which the Lomelino family radically remodelled during the 18th and 19th centuries. The drawing rooms now display furniture and paintings deeply influenced by British period style.

7 *Picnic* by Tomás da Anunciação

Picnic (above), by the founder of Portuguese Romanticism, dates from 1865. The family of the 2nd Count of Carvalhal is depicted on their Quinta do Palheiro Ferreiro estate *(see p24)*.

8 Palanquin

A 19th century palanquin, used to carry wealthy ladies around Funchal, is displayed on the ground floor. There is also a series of English satirical engravings poking fun at Funchal's well-fed priests and over-dressed officials.

9 Sugar Box Furniture

Brazilian sugar put an end to the Madeiran trade. Polished wooden boxes used to transport the sugar were made into the cupboards *(right)* seen in the basement.

10 Silver Collection

The rich collection of historic silver reflects the predominant trends in Europe from the 16th–19th century. The highlights are a pair of silver and ebony Mexican slave figures and two silver and coral British baby's rattles.

Captain Zarco: Lord of the Isles

João Gonçalves (nicknamed Zarco – "Squinter" – after he lost an eye at the Battle of Ceuta in 1415) planted the Portuguese flag on Porto Santo in 1419, and on Madeira in 1420. In 1425, he returned with people, seeds and tools to live on Madeira. Zarco ruled the island's southwestern half, while his fellow captain, Tristão Vaz, ruled the northeast from Machico. Zarco's half proved to have the better harbour, which became the island's capital. He died in 1467, at the ripe age of 80.

Left **Lower choir** Middle **17th-century carpet tiles, Santa Clara Church** Right **Upper choir**

TOP 10 Convento de Santa Clara, Funchal

1 Gateway
The arms of the Order of St Francis are carved on the 17th-century stone roundel above the ancient wooden doors of the convent gateway. Ring the bell here to enter. *Calçada de Santa Clara 15 • Map N2 • 291 742 602 • Open 10am–noon & 3–5pm Mon–Sat • Admission and guided tour €2 (under 12s free)*

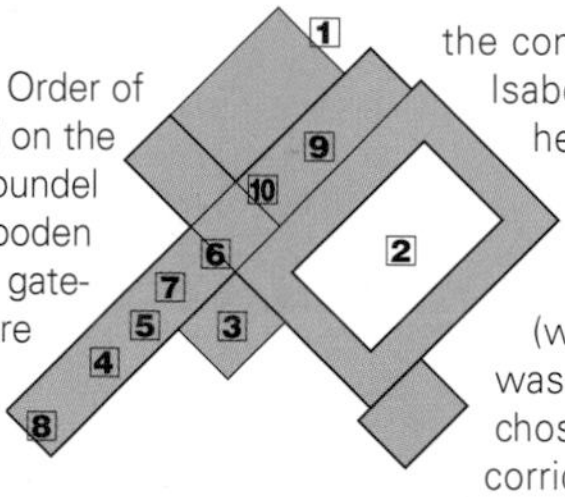

Santa Clara Convent

2 Cloister
This peaceful spot provided access to chapels and oratories, where the nuns could pass the day in prayer. From here, you can admire the cupola of the convent's bell tower, decorated with rare 17th-century blue, white and gold ceramic tiles.

3 Abbess's Grave
A gravestone with Gothic script marks the burial place of the convent's first abbess, Isabel de Noronha, and her sister, Constança. As a sign of their humility, these high-born ladies (whose grandfather was Zarco – *see p36*) chose to be buried in a corridor where nuns would walk across their graves each day.

Cloister

4 Upper Choir
Green Moorish tiles cover the floor of this long room, with its *alfarge* (knotwork) ceiling and gilded altar housing a statue of the Virgin. This choir was the place of daily prayer for the first community of Poor Clare nuns (the sister order to the Franciscans), who came to Santa Clara from Portugal in 1497.

5 Lower Choir
The lower choir is lined with wooden choir stall chairs dating from 1736, carved with winged cherubs and amusing animal heads. The painted throne was reserved for the use of the bishop and the head of the Franciscan order when either visited the convent.

6 Grille
Through the iron grille set in the eastern wall of the lower choir, the congregation could hear the sweet singing of the nuns, and the nuns could hear the priest say mass. The nuns had no other contact with the outside world.

From the Quinta das Cruzes (see pp14–15), *take the Calçada do Pico towards Funchal; the convent will be on your right.*

7 Zarco Monument
A coffin-shaped box at the eastern end of the lower choir is a replica of the marble tombstone that once stood in the main chapel over Zarco's grave *(see p15)*. It was moved in 1769 because priests kept tripping over it.

8 Calvary
The large painting of the crucified Christ at the west end of the lower choir served to remind the nuns that their hardships were as nothing compared with his sufferings. Even more poignant is the realistic 17th-century wooden statue of Christ laid in the altar below, as if in his tomb.

9 Church
The public part of the church is covered in decorative 17th-century carpet tiles of great intricacy. The magnificent silver tabernacle on the altar dates from 1671.

10 Monuments
At the back of the church, the stone sarcophagus resting on crouching lions marks the grave of Zarco's son-in-law, Martim Mendes de Vasconcelos (d.1493). Zarco himself (who died in 1467 – *see p14 & p36*) lies buried in front of the high altar, but his tomb slab is hidden beneath a modern wood floor.

Santa Clara Church

Santa Clara Convent is surrounded by high walls, built to shield the nuns from prying eyes, and to keep them focused on their religious duties without the distractions of the outside world. In the past, the only part of the convent open to the public was the church, with its magnificent silver tabernacle, dating from 1671, and its wooden altar, painted to imitate marble and gold. Because of its beauty and serenity, Santa Clara Church is a very popular choice for weddings.

Top 10 Dates in Santa Clara's History

1. 1476: convent founded
2. 1493: church completed
3. 1497: nuns move in
4. 1566: nuns flee pirates
5. 1671: tabernacle unveiled
6. 1736: choir stalls carved
7. 1797: artists paint church
8. 1834: Portugal bans religious orders
9. 1890: last nun dies
10. 1927: school founded

Bell Tower
The minaret-like bell tower reflects the cultural influence of Moorish Seville, where the tiles decorating the onion-shaped dome were made.

High altar with silver tabernacle, Santa Clara Church

TOP 10 Mercado dos Lavradores, Funchal

The bustling and colourful Mercado dos Lavradores is more than just a market; it is one of the social hubs of Madeira, a meeting place for people from all over the island, who come from the country by bus to shop and to sell their wares. The prices charged here are cheaper than those found in most of the supermarkets that are springing up all over Madeira – and who could resist buying fresh fruit, flowers or herbs from stallholders who make such efforts in creating their colourful displays?

Wickerwork, ground floor, Mercado dos Lavradores

For a tasty morsel, head for the hole-in-the-wall bars found around the outside of the market hall.

Visit the fish market in the morning. A lift situated near the ground floor entrance allows wheelchair access to the upper terrace, which has an open-air café.

- *Rua Profetas*
- *Map P4*
- *291 214 080*
- *Open 8am–7pm Mon–Thu, 7am–8pm Fri, 7am–2pm Sat*
- *Free*

Top 10 Features

1. The Market Hall
2. Leda and the Swan
3. Tile Pictures
4. Flower Sellers
5. Ground Floor
6. Cobbler
7. Fruit and Veg
8. Herbalist
9. Fish Market
10. Butchers and Bars

1 The Market Hall

This Art Deco hall was designed in 1937 by Edmundo Tavares (1892–1983). Though built from modern materials, its colours echo the grey and rust-red basalt of traditional Madeiran architecture.

2 Leda and the Swan

To the right of the entrance porch, a tile picture shows the market as it was at the turn of the 20th century *(above)*, with stalls under canvas awnings and stallholders in traditional costume. The fountain in the picture, topped by a marble statue of *Leda and the Swan*, has survived and is now in the town hall courtyard *(see p42)*.

3 Tile Pictures

More tile pictures adorn the entrance porch. The work of artist João Rodrigues, made in 1940, depicts stallholders and the coat of arms of Funchal (featuring five sugar cones in a cross).

4 Flower Sellers

Today's flower sellers still wear traditional clothes. These are as colourful and eye-catching as their tropical orchids, bird-of-paradise plants, lilies and flamingo flowers *(below)*.

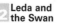

5 Ground Floor

In the arcades surrounding the central courtyard, you can shop for leather bags and wickerwork, *fado* tapes, Madeira wine and honey cake. Farmers up from the country for the day sell bread, bunches of herbs and seasonal fruits from upturned crates.

6 Cobbler

You can buy handmade and hard-wearing Madeiran-style ankle boots *(left)* and stylish leather sandals from Sousa e Sousa. The stall of this cobbler, shaped to resemble a traditional A-framed house *(see p76)*, is located on the right-hand side of the entrance.

7 Fruit and Veg

Upstairs is the domain of the fruit and vegetable sellers, packed with colourful and sweet-smelling local produce. As you negotiate the narrow aisles, don't be surprised to be offered a free slice of mango, passion fruit or blood-red tomarillo as you pass, in the hope that you will linger and buy.

8 Herbalist

On the first floor near the stairs, one stall is devoted to fresh and dried herbs, all carefully labelled. There are bunches of feverfew for headaches, and fennel and eucalyptus sweets to soothe a cold.

9 Fish Market

If the fruit stalls are a taste of the Garden of Eden, the noisy fish market *(right)*, in the basement, looks like a scene from hell, with its knife-wielding stallholders in blood-stained aprons, hacking into tuna and *espada* fish.

10 Butchers and Bars

The butchers' shops, selling fresh, cooked and dried meat and sausages, are in a separate area reached from streets around the market hall. Ringing the perimeter of the hall are hole-in-the-wall bars, where shoppers and market workers snack on little dishes of garlic-flavoured beans, salty olives or sweet custard pastries.

The Fruits of Madeira

In Funchal's market, even the commonplace can take you by surprise: the tiny honey-scented bananas, no bigger than your finger, are the best you will ever taste. Ignore shiny imported apples and tomatoes in favour of flavoursome varieties that have been grown on the island for centuries. Now is your chance to taste lantern-shaped *pitanga* (Brazilian cherries), sugar cane, prickly pears, loquats, custard apples, guava, pawpaw, passion fruit, pomegranate and quince – all grown locally.

TOP 10 Jardim Botânico, Funchal

As well as being a place where avid plant lovers can learn all about the astonishing range of plants that thrive in Madeira's warm and humid climate, this is also a great spot just to relax and enjoy the visual richness of the immaculately maintained flower beds. The gardens occupy the grounds of an estate that once belonged to the Reid family (founders of the world-renowned Belmond Reid's Palace) and, with a practised eye for a good building site, they chose to build their mansion on a sunny slope blessed with panoramic views.

The outdoor café in the Jardim Botânico

There is a café in the grounds set around a series of pretty lotus- and lily-filled ponds.

Some of the best views are to be had from the "Lovers' Cave" at the topmost point of the garden.

Entry to the Jardim Botânico also includes admission to the Jardim dos Loiros, or Parrot Park *(see p53)*. Orchid fans shouldn't miss the Jardim Orquídea *(see p56)*, a short, if steep, walk away.

A cable car gets you to Monte *(see pp26–7)* in around 10 minutes.

- *Quinta do Bom Sucesso, Caminho do Meio*
- *Map H5*
- *291 211 200*
- *www.sra.pt*
- *Open 9am–5:30pm daily*
- *Admission €5.50 (under 6s free)*

Top 10 Features

1. Natural History Museum
2. Native Plants
3. Valley View
4. Cacti and Succulents
5. Carpet Bedding
6. Economic Plants
7. Scientific Plants
8. Topiary Garden
9. Coastal Plants
10. Parrot Park

1 Natural History Museum

The Quinta do Bom Sucesso ("Mansion of Good Fortune") *(below)*, built in the late 19th century by the Reid family *(see p37 & p112)*, was bought by the Madeiran government in 1952. In 1982, the Natural History Museum opened here.

2 Native Plants

So many plants have been introduced to the island that it is useful to be reminded of native species. Those growing in beds alongside the museum *(above)* include bold and colourful Madeiran geraniums and giant golden buttercups.

3 Valley View

The western edge of the garden (furthest from the entrance) has views over the green, canyon-like João Gomes Valley *(below)*. Though crossed by a road bridge, this is an important wildlife corridor. Huge, ancient and gnarled parasol pines, with twisted branches and scaly bark, cling to the rocks alongside the *miradouro* (viewing point) that overlooks the valley.

The Botanical Gardens are 3 km (2 miles) northeast of Funchal, on the route of town buses 30 and 31.

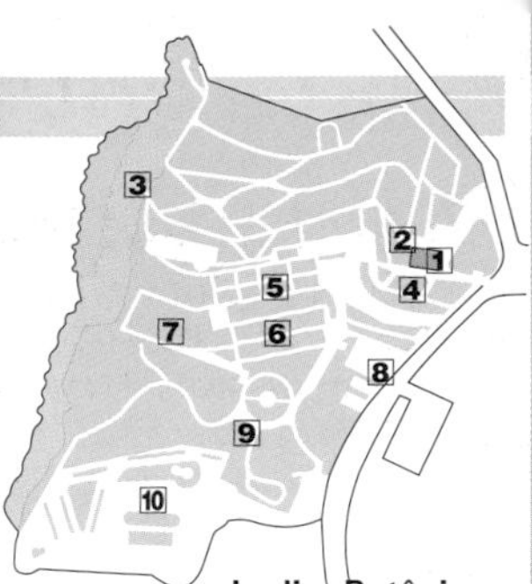

Jardim Botânico

4 Cacti and Succulents

This part of the garden is popular with children for its Wild West look *(above)* and for the many spiders that use the thorns of the cacti as supports for their intricate webs.

5 Carpet Bedding

The purple, red, green, yellow, white and gold diamonds, lozenges and circles of this much-photographed part of the garden *(left)* demonstrate the richness and variety of colour to be found just in the leaves of plants.

6 Economic Plants

If you cannot tell a mango tree from an avocado, this is the place to learn. The plants grown here are used for food, fibre, oil or dye. Among them are several whose names we know but may never have seen – such as coffee, cocoa, sugar cane, cotton and papaya.

7 Scientific Plants

Staff carry out research using the plants grown in this section to understand plant taxonomy, reproductive biology and ecology.

8 Topiary Garden

This knot garden *(above)* is made of clipped box, and planted with shrubs that can be cut into spirals, pyramids, chess pieces and animal shapes.

9 Coastal Plants

Near to this area, where the palm trees and cycads collection is situated, is a small group of Madeiran indigenous and endemic plant species. These hardy plants manage to thrive on rocky cliffs or along the shoreline.

10 Parrot Park

The closer you get to the southern part of the garden, the less you will be able to avoid the squawks of the rare and exotic birds that are housed in the Parrot Park *(left)*.

Dragon Trees

If ever a plant looked like its name, the dragon tree *(Dracaena draco)* is it. The fleshlike branches have scaly grey bark that looks and feels reptilian, while the leaves are like claws or talons. When cut, the tree "bleeds" a vivid red sap which sets to form a resinous gum known as Dragon's Blood, once highly prized as a dye (it turns cloth purple). Long before Portugal colonized Madeira, sailors came here to harvest the sap of these strange trees, which still grow wild in Madeira, the Canary Islands and Cape Verde.

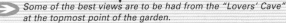

Some of the best views are to be had from the "Lovers' Cave" at the topmost point of the garden.

Left **Madeiran geranium** Middle **Pride of Madeira** Right **Giant buttercups**

TOP 10 Plants on Madeira

1 Madeiran Geranium
The Madeiran geranium, also known as cranesbill *(Geranium maderense)*, has become a popular garden plant all over Europe because of its shrubby stature, feathery leaves and large purple-veined magenta flowers.

2 Pride of Madeira
Pride of Madeira *(Echium candicans)* is almost the island's symbol. Blooming with an abundance of long-lasting powder-blue flower spikes at exactly the time of year (from December to March) when other flowers are shy, it adorns the island's roadsides, notably around the airport.

3 Lily-of-the-valley Tree
You could pass this shrub (*Clethra arborea*, or *folhado* in Portuguese) nine months out of twelve and not even notice it, but from August to October it is a stunner, hung all over with sweet-smelling clusters of bell-like flowers of purest white.

Madeiran juniper

4 Tree Heath
Related to heather, and with similar pink bell-like flowers, Madeira's tree heaths *(Erica arborea)* can grow to a quite prodigious size; a carbonized tree heath trunk in Madeira's Natural History Museum *(see p20)* probably lived for several hundred years. Tree heath branches are used locally for fencing and windbreaks.

5 Giant Buttercups
Madeira's subtropical climate seems to encourage plants to turn into giants. Here, Poinsettias grow 4 m (12 ft) tall, and heaths are trees rather than shrubs. This tall shrubby buttercup (*Ranunculus cortusifolia*) is a very handsome plant that looks good anywhere.

6 Scented Bay
The essential flavouring ingredient in Madeira's national dish, *espetada* (beef kebabs), is the scented bay (*Lauras novocanariensis*, or *loureiro* in Portuguese). It has aromatic evergreen leaves and grows abundantly in the wild.

7 Madeiran Juniper
Confusingly called *cedro* (cedar) in Portuguese, the dark wood of the Madeiran juniper has a rich patina that can be readily seen in the knotwork ceilings of Funchal Cathedral *(see p9)*, Santa Clara Convent *(see p16)* and the church in Calheta *(see p82)*.

8 Ironwood

Apollonius barbujana (in Portuguese, *barbusano*) is one of the main constituents of Madeira's native evergreen forest. Its billowing clouds of fresh lime-green leaves contrast with the deep green of previous years' growth.

9 Stink Laurel

The Portuguese took a heavy toll of the huge and ancient laurel trees (*Ocotea foetens*, or *til* in Portuguese) after they arrived on the island in 1420. Felled trunks were shipped to Portugal and Spain for shipbuilding; the ships of the Spanish Armada were largely built from this wood.

10 Madeiran Mahogany

Madeira's museums are full of fine furniture made from *vinhático (Persea indica)*, the mahogany-like wood that grows to a great height and girth in the woods. So valuable and costly was sugar in the 15th century that it was shipped to Europe in chests made of this wood.

Top 10 Wild Plants to Spot on a Walk

1. Viper's bugloss
2. Saucer plant (House leek)
3. Navelwort
4. Downy thistle
5. Shrubby sow thistle
6. Ice plant
7. Bilberry
8. Foxglove
9. Dog violet
10. Fleabane

Madeira: World Heritage Site

The primeval woodland that cloaks much of Madeira's mountainous interior is the remnant of the scented laurel forest that covered much of southern Europe until the last Ice Age (which ended around 10,000 years ago). Only on Madeira, the Canaries, the Azores and in tropical west Africa was the climate warm enough for these subtropical trees and shrubs to survive. Known in Portuguese as laurissilva *(laurel wood), they are a precious link with the past. UNESCO designated a large area of the island's natural forest as a protected World Heritage Site in December 1999.*

Primeval woodland

For more Madeiran flowers **See p45**

TOP 10 Quinta do Palheiro Ferreiro

The unmistakably English character of the Quinta do Palheiro Ferreiro was stamped on the estate by its first owner, the wealthy Count of Carvalhal, whose love of English landscapes led him to include woodland and grassy meadows when the estate was laid out in 1804. Bought by John Blandy, an English wine merchant, in 1885, the Quinta has remained in the same family ever since, greatly enriched by the plants that Mildred Blandy imported from China, Japan and her native South Africa.

Pink flowers and leaves of the cymbidium orchid

The Tea House, serving delicious home-made cakes, stands at the lower end of the garden, bordering an area of the estate, which is now run as a golf course *(see p48)*.

A Rose Garden, near the Chapel, includes traditional roses and also newer varieties brought in from the UK.

Visitors should note that the Old House is open to hotel guests only.

- *Caminho da Quinta do Palheiro 32, São Gonçalo*
- *Map H5*
- *291 793 044*
- *www.palheirogardens.com*
- *9am–5:30pm daily*
- *Admission €10.50 (children 15–17s €4, under 15s free)*

Top 10 Features

1. The Long Avenue
2. Stream Garden
3. The Sunken Garden
4. The Chapel
5. Long Borders
6. The Terrace
7. The Old House
8. Lady's Garden
9. Hell Valley
10. Camellia Walk

1 The Long Avenue

Plane trees and giant camellias, many planted 200 years ago, line the avenue. The crimson, pink and white flowers are at their best from November to April, before the white arum lilies and pretty blue agapanthus take over.

2 Stream Garden

The stream you cross to enter the garden is fed by a spring. Lined by azaleas, rhododendrons and scarlet tritonias, and crossed by ornamental bridges, it attracts bathing robins and blackbirds.

3 The Sunken Garden

Water lilies fill the little pool at the centre of this pretty garden *(above)*. Tall cypresses mark its corners; topiary shapes flank its four sets of stone steps. In the borders, gazanias mix with beetroot-red house leeks.

4 The Chapel

The striking Baroque chapel has Venetian-style windows and a plasterwork ceiling depicting Christ being baptized in the River Jordan by John the Baptist.

The Quinta is 8 km (5 miles) from the centre of Funchal, on the route of town buses 36, 36a, 37 and 47.

5 Long Borders

Typically English herbaceous border plants, such as delphiniums and day lilies, are mixed with tender and exotic orchids, and angel's trumpets (daturas). Climbing roses and jasmine are draped over arches so that you catch the heady scent as you pass.

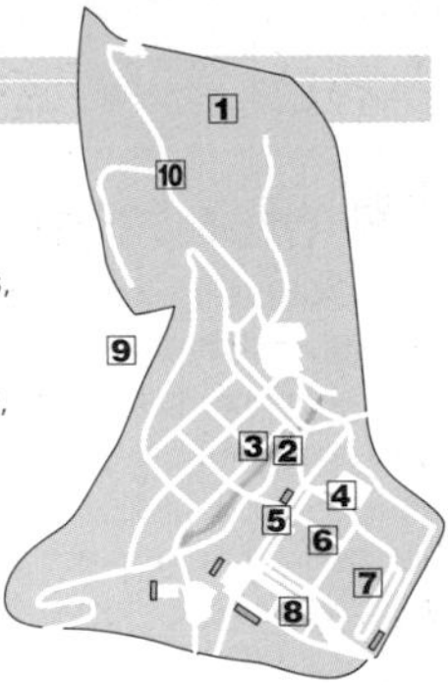

Quinta do Palheiro Ferreiro

6 The Terrace

Paved with tiny sea-worn pebbles, the terrace offers a good view of the house (no admission) that John Blandy built in 1885, successfully blending English and Madeiran architectural styles.

7 The Old House

Now a luxurious hotel *(see p113)*, the Casa Velha was originally a hunting lodge. Archduchess Leopoldina of Austria stayed here on her way to marry Pedro I of Brazil in 1817.

9 Hell Valley

Despite its name, this valley is a delightful tangle of bamboo, tree ferns, native woodland and creepers, with an understorey of beautiful acanthus plants.

8 Lady's Garden

The *Jardim da Senhora* (above) has topiary nesting birds and vintage trees, including a grand old Madeiran *til* tree *(see p23)*, two Canary pines and a weeping *Saphora japonica*, whose corkscrew limbs and delicate leaves cascade to the ground to form a natural green veil.

10 Camellia Walk

Look out for the stone circle called Avista Navios ("Place for Viewing Ships"), where there is a clear view all the way down to the harbour.

The Blandy Family

The first John Blandy (1783–1855) arrived in 1807 as quartermaster in General Beresford's army, which had been posted to Madeira to defend the island against attack from Napoleon. Blandy returned in 1811, and made his fortune supplying the ships that called at Funchal's busy port. His eldest son, Charles Ridpath, bought up all existing stocks of wine on the island when mildew caused grape harvests to fail in 1852. This bold move enabled the family to dominate the wine trade from then on.

The name Palheiro Ferreiro literally means "blacksmith's hut". Perhaps long ago a blacksmith chose this spot for his forge.

Top 10 Monte

Like the hill stations of colonial India, Monte (literally, "Mount") developed in the late 18th century as a genteel and healthy retreat from the heat, smells, noise and commercial activity of the capital. Funchal's suburbs now spread their tentacles all the way up to Monte, but there is still a sense of escaping from the city and entering a world set apart. The cool, clear air is filled with birdsong. Few cars intrude onto the cobbled streets, and lush gardens are everywhere – lushest of all, the extraordinary Monte Palace Tropical Garden (see pp28–9).

Monte Palace Garden

You can get to Monte from Funchal by taxi, or by buses 20 or 21. The most exhilarating way, however, is to go up by cable car, from Funchal's Old Town or the Jardim Botânico *(see pp20–23)*. You can return by the traditional Monte toboggan ... or on foot; the Caminho do Monte is a steep but direct road into Funchal, passing through some older suburbs of the city. To get onto it, just follow the toboggan run.

- *Map H5*
- *Nossa Senhora do Monte Church. 291 783 877. Open 9am–6pm Mon–Sat, 8am–1pm Sun. Free*
- *Quinta Jardins do Imperador. Camhino do Pico. 291 780 460. Open 9:30am–5:30pm Mon–Sat. Admission (to garden only) €6 (children €3, under 12s free)*
- *Toboggan run. Open 9am–6pm Mon–Sat. Fare €25 (€30 for two people, €45 for three people)*

Top 10 Features

1. Toboggan Run
2. House of the Pilgrims
3. Church Steps
4. Nossa Senhora do Monte
5. Quinta do Monte
6. Cable Car Station
7. Monte Palace Tropical Garden
8. Fountain Square
9. Quinta Jardins do Imperador
10. Parque do Monte

1 Toboggan Run

Madeira's toboggans are steered by smartly dressed *carreiros* (toboggan drivers) in straw boaters on the 2-km (1-mile) trip from Monte to Livra-mento.

2 House of the Pilgrims

This 18th-century building is used as a cultural centre. It houses an exhibition of paintings devoted to Emperor Charles I.

3 Church Steps

On the Feast of the Assumption (15 August), pilgrims climb on their knees up the steep steps to Monte's church to pay homage to the statue of the Virgin, which they believe was presented by the Virgin herself when she appeared to a shepherd girl in the 15th century.

The entrance to Monte Palace Tropical Garden lies to the south of Nossa Senhora do Monte, near the start point for the toboggan run.

4 Nossa Senhora do Monte

Our Lady of Monte was inaugurated in 1818, replacing a 15th-century chapel built by Adam Ferreira (the first person to be born on Madeira – along with his twin sister, Eve). The church houses the tomb of Emperor Charles I of Austria.

5 Quinta do Monte

Converted into a fine hotel *(see p113)*, the 19th-century Quinta do Monte sits in beautiful terraced grounds, open to the public during the day. At the heart of the garden is the Baroque chapel of the Quinta do Monte, and within the pretty garden gazebo, is a small café, serving teas.

6 Cable Car Station

The cable car's sleek steel-and-glass terminus is the only modern building in Monte. Along its route up the wild João Gomes Valley, you can see examples of many protected species of native trees and flowers.

7 Monte Palace Tropical Garden

Lakes, waterfalls and an engaging museum have earned the Monte Palace Tropical Garden *(see pp28–9)* a name among the world's most beautiful botanical gardens.

8 Fountain Square

Set in a natural amphitheatre shaded by giant plane trees, Monte's main square is beautifully paved with sea-rounded cobbles. The square is named after the marble fonte of 1897 *(left)*. In its back wall is a niche housing a statue of the Virgin of Monte – a copy of the one in the church.

9 Quinta Jardins do Imperador

Just south of Monte (first right going downhill toward Funchal) is the beautiful mansion where Charles I lived in exile. The romantic knot gardens and lake enclose the Malakoff Tower, which houses a café.

10 Parque do Monte

This public park was laid out in 1894 beneath the stone railway viaduct now draped in climbing *Monstera deliciosa* plants. Cobbled paths thread in and out of the arches into a valley full of hydrangeas, tree ferns and massed agapanthus.

Emperor Charles I (1887–1922)

Charles I was ruler of an empire stretching from Vienna to Budapest. When it collapsed with Austria's defeat in World War I, he fled into exile, choosing the tiny island of Madeira because of his fond memories of holidays spent here. His happiness was short-lived: arriving on the island in November 1921, he succumbed to pneumonia and died in April 1922. Following Pope John Paul II's decision to beatify him, pilgrims now regularly visit his tomb in Monte's church.

Left ***Nativity*, detail** Middle **Swan Lake** Right **Japanese Garden**

Monte Palace Tropical Garden

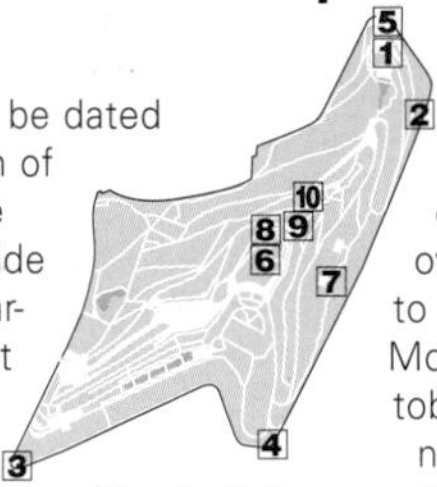

Monte Palace Tropical Garden

1 Ancient Olives

Ancient trees can be dated by their girth; the girth of the three ancient olive trees growing just inside the entrance to the garden is at least as great as their height. Probably planted in 300 BC by the Romans, they are part of a group of 40 ancient olive trees rescued from the Alentejo in Portugal when the huge Alqueva Dam (Europe's largest artificial lake) was built.

2 Tile Pictures

The 40 tile panels lining the main avenue depict scenes from Portuguese history, from the reign of Afonso Henriques, who took Lisbon from the Moors in 1147, to Madeiran autonomy within Portugal in 1976.

Painted tiles near Swan Lake

3 Belvedere

The balcony at the south-western corner of the garden overlooks the road down to Funchal frequented by Monte's traditional toboggans. The road is now covered in asphalt, and the drivers have to struggle to make the toboggans travel at any speed. There are plans to restore the original cobbles so that the ride can once again live up to its description by the writer Ernest Hemingway as "the most exhilarating ride in the world".

4 Elephant's Foot Trees

North of the café at the bottom of the garden, you will find the aptly-named elephant's foot trees from Mexico.

5 Monte Palace Museum

This modern museum houses an amazing collection of minerals and gems, plus many beautiful Zimbabwean sculptures dating from the 1950s and 1960s.

6 Swan Lake

The jar stands alongside a small lake enlivened by ducks, swans and koi carp, as well as fountains and fern-filled grottoes. The walls are decorated with Art Deco tiles rescued from demolished buildings in Lisbon. One advertises Japanese-style parasols *(left)*, another wicker furniture and oriental carpets.

For more details, visit www.montepalace.com

7 Madeiran Flora

To the left of the main path is an area devoted to plants indigenous to Madeira's *laurisilva* forest *(see p23)*, including the thornless *Ilex perado* (Madeiran holly) and *Euphorbia piscatoria* (known in Portuguese as *Figueira do inferno* – "the fig from hell"), whose poisonous sap was once used for stunning fish.

8 Limestone Nativity

On the terrace above the lake, look for the 16th-century *Nativity* carved in fine-grained limestone by the Renaissance artist Jean de Rouen. The panels depicting shepherds and their flocks are especially charming.

9 Tiles and Sculpture

The terraces are also decorated with 17th- and 18th-century tile "wainscots" painted with cherubs and religious scenes, salvaged from demolished convents and chapels around Portugal. Note, too, the fine Italian Romanesque well head, with its amusing motto, "The more you give, the less you have to worry about!"

10 Japanese Garden

Guarded by leonine marble temple dogs, the Japanese Garden's lush green vegetation contrasts sharply with the bright red of the gardens' bridges and traditional Japanese archways.

Top 10 Other Quintas to Visit

1. Quinta da Boa Vista
2. Quinta do Bom Sucesso
3. Quinta das Cruzes
4. Quinta do Furão
5. Quinta Jardins do Imperador
6. Quinta Magnólia
7. Quinta do Monte
8. Quinta do Palheiro Ferreiro
9. Quinta da Palmeira
10. Quinta Vigia

Monte Palace

Monte Palace was a more modest villa in the 18th century, when the estate belonged to the English consul Charles Murray. Later expanded into a hotel, it now belongs to the José Berardo Foundation, an educational and environmental concern endowed by a Madeira-born entrepreneur who made his fortune extracting gold in South Africa. Outside, there are sculptures, as well as peacocks and "Ali Baba" pots. Caminho do Monte • Map H5 • 291 780 800 • Gardens: open 9:30am–6pm daily; Museum: open 10am–4:30pm daily. Admission €10 (under 14s free). Palace closed to the public

Monte Palace

For more on the Quintas listed above **See pp14–15, p20, pp24–5, p26, p27, p44–45, p59**

TOP 10 Curral das Freiras

The easiest way to get a feel for the sublime grandeur of Madeira's mountainous interior is to visit Curral das Freiras ("Nuns' Refuge"), the hidden valley used as a hideaway by the nuns of Santa Clara Convent (see pp16–17) *whenever pirates attacked the island. (The same name is also given to the little village that now nestles there.) From such a beautiful spot, they must have returned to their city convent with a heavy heart. Visiting in 1825, H N Coleridge (the nephew of the English poet) described the Curral as "one of the great sights of the world".*

View of the landscape around Pico Grande

At Sabores do Curral *(see p79)*, delicious local cuisine is served on a terrace with spectacular mountain views.

Many tour companies in Funchal offer half-day trips to Curral das Freiras, often in combination with Monte *(see p26)* or Câmara de Lobos *(see p75)*. Most of these trips go only as far as Eira do Serrado, the viewing point above the village.

Curral das Freiras is on the route of Carros de São Gonçalo bus 81.

- *Map G4*
- *www.horariosdofunchal.pt*

Top 10 Features

1. Eira do Serrado
2. Miradouro
3. Igreja Matriz
4. View to the East
5. View to the North
6. View to the West
7. Footpath
8. Road
9. Chestnut Woods
10. Village

1 Eira do Serrado

Admiring this vista from Eira do Serrado *(right)* is as much a part of a visit to Curral das Freiras as the descent into the village itself. There is a hotel and restaurant, so if you fall in love with the romantic view, you can stay for lunch or dinner, or even spend the night *(see p116)*.

2 Miradouro

From the car park in front of the hotel, a short footpath leads up to a *miradouro*, or viewing point *(below)*, high above the Socorridos Valley. From here, the village far below looks like "Shangri-La" – the utopia of James Hilton's novel *Lost Horizon* (1933).

3 Igreja Matriz

This church dates from the early 19th century. On the last Sunday in August, a statue of the church's patron saint is carried through streets festooned with colourful paper flowers.

4 View to the East

Because of its cauldron-like shape, early explorers thought the Curral das Freiras, with its dramatic cliffs rising sheer to the east, was a collapsed volcano. In fact, the circular form is purely the result of millions of years of river and rain erosion.

5 View to the North
To the north beyond the village, a road heads up the valley, currently ending just after it disappears from view. There are plans to tunnel through the island's mountainous centre and take the road to the north coast, endangering the tranquillity of the Curral.

6 View to the West
To the west is a serrated ridge with three prominent peaks: Pico do Cavalho, Pico do Serradhino and, highest of all at 1,654 m (5,427 ft), Pico Grande. Beyond, the next great valley runs from Ribeira Brava to São Vicente via the Encumeada Pass *(see p81)*.

7 Footpath
To prolong your visit to the Curral, you can walk down to the village along the cobbled footpath *(above)* that begins in the car park. The path has 52 bends; at the bottom, turn right and walk uphill to the village. You can return by bus 81.

8 Road
Until the road was built in 1969, the only way in and out of the valley was the footpath. The old road is now closed. Instead, a modern tunnelled highway connects this picturesque destination with the rest of the island.

9 Chestnut Woods
The descent to the village takes you through chestnut woods *(left)*. The trees bear white, sweetly scented flower stems in August, and produce edible chestnuts in October. Lower down, there is natural *laurisilva* forest *(see p23)*. In June, look out for wild orchids.

10 Village
The café owners will urge you to try their chestnut dishes *(right)* – roasted salted chestnuts, rich chestnut soup and sweet chestnut cake. Sample, too, the delicious chestnut liqueur *castanha*.

Pirates Ahoy!
Pirates were a serious menace in the early history of Madeira, which is why Funchal has no less than three forts. The worst attack occurred in 1566, when the French pirate Bertrand de Montluc, landed at Praia Formosa with 1,000 men and plundered the city's churches and mansions over a 15-day period, massacring all who stood in their way. Montluc gained nothing from his piracy, as he died from a wound he received in the attack.

Top 10 Pico do Arieiro

Mountaineering equipment is not needed to get to the top of Madeira's third highest peak, because a road takes you all the way from the bustle of Funchal to the silence of the summit in less than an hour. The mountain top provides a viewing platform from which to look out over the multiple peaks and ravines of the island's central mountains. Standing aloft here, you have a chance to study the astonishing range of rock formations left over from the violent volcanic upheavals that led to the creation of the island.

The view from Pico do Arieiro

There is a convenient café at the summit.

Pico do Arieiro can be wrapped in cloud for much of the day. The best times of day for fine weather are before 10am and after 5pm. Alternatively, you can take a chance on the clouds clearing for your visit. It is often possible to drive up through the clouds and emerge to find the summit basking in sunshine.

Even at the height of summer, it can be cold and windy at the summit, and in winter, ice and snow are common. It is best to take warm and waterproof clothing.

• *Map G4*

Top 10 Features

1. Ecological Park
2. Ice House
3. Sheep Pens
4. Trig Point
5. Footpath
6. Café
7. View to the West
8. Volcanic Dykes
9. View to the East
10. Wildlife

1 Ecological Park

Some 12 km (7 miles) out of Funchal on the drive up, you pass the entrance to the Ecological Park, where primeval forest has been restored. With its viewing points and glades, it is popular for picnics.

2 Ice House

This igloo-shaped building *(above)*, 2 km (1 mile) south of the peak, is called Poço da Neve ("Snow Well"), and was built in 1813 by an Italian ice cream maker. Ice from pits like this one provided wealthy hotel guests with "snow water" in the heat of summer.

3 Sheep Pens

Livestock has been banned from the Ecological Park to allow Madeiran bilberry and heather to thrive, but sheep and goats graze around the summit and their circular pens are seen here.

4 Trig Point

A short scramble up from the café brings you to the actual summit, 1,818 m (5,965 ft) above sea level. It is marked by a concrete post used for measuring altitude and location *(below)*.

Buses do not go to the peak, but taxis will take you there and back for a fixed fee.

5 Footpath

A footpath *(right)* links four main peaks and is one of the island's most exciting walks. It should not be attempted unless you are properly equipped for challenging mountain conditions (including sudden storms, tunnels and unprotected drops). A large yellow sign marks the start of the path. Walk the first 100 m (110 yards) or so for fine views back to the summit.

6 Café

The photographs on the walls of the summit café show the peak at sunset, at sunrise and in snow. They might well tempt you to make return visits to enjoy the colours of the sky at dusk or dawn, or to view the night sky away from the glare of city lights.

7 View to the West

The view westward from the summit *(above)* takes in the entire central mountain range, with its succession of knife-edge peaks as far as the eye can see. The predominant colours are the fiery reds, rust browns, blacks and purples of oxidized volcanic rocks, in a scene more like the surface of Mars than the Earth.

8 Volcanic Dykes

Another distinctive feature of the view to the west and south is a series of parallel grey outcrops, resembling the Great Wall of China, that follow the contours of the landscape. These are, in fact, vertical seams of hard volcanic rock that have resisted the erosive forces of rain, frost and wind.

9 View to the East

The view to the east looks down over the green wooded slopes of the island's indigenous forest *(see p23)*. On a clear day, it is possible to see the meadow landscape of Santo da Serra, and the island's long rocky tail, the Ponta de São Lourenço, curving off into the distance.

10 Wildlife

Even on the bare, dry rocks of Madeira's high peaks, plants find a niche wherever a crack provides shelter and moisture. Among the gorse *(right)* and heather, you can spot grasshoppers and the well-camouflaged native grayling butterfly.

Island Origins

Madeira's long, slow birth began 18 million years ago, as lava burst up through the ocean floor to create layer upon layer of basaltic rock. It took 15 million years for Pico do Arieiro to reach its present height. For another 2.25 million years, further eruptions spilled lava sideways from the island's central core, creating the flatter plains of the Paúl da Serra to the west and Santo da Serra to the east. Volcanic activity did not finally cease until 6,450 years ago, when the caves at São Vicente *(see p81)* were formed.

Left **Belmond Reid's Palace** Right **Statue of Tristão Vaz Teixeira in Machico**

TOP 10 Moments in History

1 Island Formation

Twenty million years ago, the islands of the Madeiran group began to emerge from the sea (first Porto Santo, then Madeira and the Ilhas Desertas). Pockets of fertile soil were created as storms eroded the softer layers of volcanic ash. Slowly, the island came to life, as seeds excreted by visiting birds took root and spread.

2 Early Visitors

Sailors visited Madeira to gather sap from dragon trees for use in dying clothes. Mentioned in the *Natural History* of Pliny the Elder (AD 23–79), Madeira first appears on the Medici Map of 1351, as "Isola de Lolegname" ("Wooded Isle").

3 Zarco Arrives

Prince Henry "the Navigator" (1394–1460), third son of King John I of Portugal, realized how valuable Madeira was to sailors exploring the Atlantic Ocean. He sent João Gonçalves Zarco (1387–1467) *(see p15)* to the islands. Zarco landed on Porto Santo, and returned in 1420 to claim Madeira for Portugal.

4 Colonization

Portuguese colonization of Madeira began in 1425, when Zarco returned to govern the southwestern half from Funchal. Tristão Vaz Teixeira controlled the northeastern half, and Bartolomeu Perestrelo governed Porto Santo. Machico was initially the capital, but Funchal had a better harbour and gained city status in 1508.

5 Prosperity

By 1470, Madeira's early settlers were exporting wheat, dyestuffs, wine and timber, but sugar produced the biggest profits. Trading with London, Antwerp, Venice and Genoa, the island bloomed for 150 years as Europe's main sugar producer, channelling the profits into building and art.

6 Wine

Quick profits and wealth became a thing of the past once Caribbean and Brazilian sugar hit European markets in the mid-16th century. *Malvazia* (Malmsey), a rich sweet wine, then took over as Madeira's main export. It is the favourite drink of Shakespeare's roistering character Falstaff.

Prince Henry "The Navigator"

7 The British Arrive

British merchants dominated the wine trade after Charles II married the Portuguese princess Catherine of Braganza in 1662, and British (and American) taxes on Madeira wine were reduced as part of the marriage settlement. So valuable was Madeira to the British, that an armed force was sent in 1801 to prevent Napoleon from capturing it.

Preceding pages **Traditional A-framed houses, Santana**

8 Belmond Reid's Palace

Once the Napoleonic Wars were over, Madeira became a popular winter holiday destination for wealthy northern Europeans. Symbolic of the era is Belmond Reid's Palace, founded by William Reid, who arrived a poor sailor in 1836 and made a fortune renting houses to aristocratic visitors.

9 Autonomy

Madeira escaped the worst effects of the two World Wars, but by 1974, the year of Portugal's Carnation Revolution, it had become Europe's poorest region. In that year, Portugal's dictatorship was toppled in a coup by army officers. Later, celebrating soldiers had carnations stuck in their gun barrels by joyous civilians. In 1976, Madeira became largely autonomous, except for tax, foreign policy and defence.

10 Catastrophe

In 2008, Funchal celebrated its 500th anniversary as the capital of an increasingly prosperous island, but in February 2010, a devastating storm caused widespread floods. Lives were lost, and homes, roads and bridges destroyed. Funchal was particularly affected, but within weeks was functioning again thanks to the resolve of the islanders.

Catherine of Braganza

Top 10 Famous Visitors

1 Robert Machin

This shipwrecked sailor and his lover Anne of Hertford died on Madeira in the 1370s.

2 King Ladislaw III

Having lost the Battle of Varna in 1414, the former king of Poland was one of Madeira's first settlers.

3 Columbus

Columbus came as a sugar merchant in 1478–9, and returned in 1498 on his way to the New World for the last time.

4 Captain Kidd

Nobody has ever found the treasure that the pirate Captain Kidd is said to have buried on Ilhas Desertas in the 1690s.

5 Captain James Cook

The explorer called in at Madeira on his ship, the *Endeavour*, in 1768.

6 Napoleon

The vanquished French emperor bought wine at Funchal on his way to exile on St Helena in 1815.

7 Emperor Charles I

The last Austro-Hungarian emperor died in exile on Madeira in 1922 *(see p27)*.

8 George Bernard Shaw

Visiting in 1927, the Irish playwright praised his dancing instructor as "the only man who ever taught me anything".

9 Winston Churchill

Churchill wrote *The Hinge of Fate* (volume 4 of his memoirs) while staying at Reid's Hotel in 1949.

10 Margaret Thatcher

The future British prime minister, Margaret Thatcher, spent her honeymoon at the Savoy Hotel in 1951.

Left **Museu Photographia Vincentes** Right **Casa Museu Frederico de Freitas**

TOP 10 Museums

1 Museu de Arte Sacra, Funchal

Funchal's Religious Art Museum is renowned for its colourful 16th-century Flemish paintings, but also has many remarkable polychrome wooden statues *(see pp10–11)*.

Franciscan saints, Museu de Arte Sacra

2 The Old Blandy Wine Lodge, Funchal

A guided visit to this charming, cobblestoned vintage Madeira wine lodge is a heady experience involving all the senses *(see pp12–13)*.

3 Museu da Quinta das Cruzes, Funchal

This is the house where Madeira's first ruler lived when Madeira was still young – the newest addition to Portugal's growing portfolio of overseas colonies at the start of the great Age of Discovery in the 15th century. Paintings and sketches of the island's major landmarks hang on the walls of the Quinta's richly decorated rooms *(see pp14–15)*.

***Picnic* by T. da Anunciacao, Museu da Quinta das Cruzes**

4 Museu da Baleia, Caniçal

Madeira's Whale Museum welcomes visitors to a world of dolphins and whales. Interactive and 3D displays depict the evolution of these fascinating creatures. Exhibits include a whaling boat. *Rua da Pedra d'Eira • Map L4 • 291 961 858 • Open 11am–6pm Tue–Sun • Adm charge • www.museudabaleia.pt*

5 Museu Photographia Vicentes, Funchal

Founded by Vincent Gomes da Silva in 1852 (12 years after photography was invented), this photographic studio survives, complete with cameras, sets and costumes. *Rua da Carreira 43 • Map P3 • 291 225 050 • 10am–12:30pm & 2–5pm Mon–Fri • Adm charge*

6 Museu Municipal e Aquário, Funchal

This museum offers a darkened aquarium downstairs, and a study collection of stuffed fish, birds and other Madeiran wildlife upstairs. *Rua da Mouraria 31 • Map P2 • 291 229 761 • 10am–6pm Tue–Sun • Adm charge*

7 Casa Museu Frederico de Freitas, Funchal

Packed with antiques and religious paintings, this museum also has an amusing collection of teapots from all over the world. A wing is devoted to ceramic tiles, with superb early examples from long-gone Madeiran churches. *Calçada de Santa Clara 7 • Map N2 • 291 202 570 • 10am–5:30pm Tue– Sat • Adm charge*

8 Museu Henrique e Francisco Franco, Funchal

The artistic Franco brothers, painter Henrique (1883–1961) and sculptor Francisco (1855–1955), left Madeira to find fame in Lisbon and Paris. Their achievements are celebrated here. *Rua João de Deus 13 • Map N4 • 291 230 633 • 9:30am–6:30pm Mon–Fri • Adm charge*

Museu Henrique e Francisco Franco

9 Madeira Story Centre, Funchal

An interactive museum covering all aspects of the island's history. *Rua Dom Carlos I 27–29 • Map P5 • 291 000 770 • 10am–6pm daily • Adm charge*

10 Centro das Artes Casa das Mudas, Calheta

Works of artists such as Picasso and Francis Bacon have been exhibited here. *Estrada Simão Gonçalves da Câmara 37 • Map B4 • 291 820 900 • 10am–1pm & 2–6pm Tue–Sun • Adm charge*

Top 10 Museum Exhibits

1 Processional Cross
Superb Renaissance silverwork, with the Evangelists and biblical scenes in relief (Museu de Arte Sacra) *(see p10)*.

2 Max Romer Murals
Grape-harvest scenes capturing the vigour of youth and the golden light of autumn (The Old Blandy Wine Lodge) *(see p12)*.

3 Indian Miniature
The Virgin depicted as a Mogul princess (Room 1, Quinta das Cruzes) *(see p14)*.

4 Wood Sculpture
Rare tribal sculpture from Zimbabwe dating from the 1950s and 1960s (Monte Palace Museum) *(see p28)*.

5 Photo Albums
Sepia-tinted prints of 150 years of island life (Museu Photographia Vicentes).

6 Moray Eels
Sharp-fanged denizens of the deep (Museu Municipal e Aquário).

7 Winter Garden
Fern-filled, Art Nouveau glass conservatory at the Casa Museu Frederico de Freitas.

8 Boy with Cockerel
This portrait of a Madeiran peasant boy is one of Henrique Franco's best (Museu Henrique e Francisco Franco).

9 Portraits of Columbus
Paintings and drawings of Christopher Columbus (1451–1506) line the walls of the legendary explorer's house (Casa Museu Cristóvão Colombo) *(see p95)*.

10 Scrimshaws
Whalebones carved and etched in the days before hunting whales was illegal (Museu da Baleia) *(see p87)*.

Left *Last Supper* São Salvador Right Funchal Cathedral (Sé)

Top 10 Churches

1 Funchal Cathedral (Sé)
Funchal cathedral set the pattern for the island's other churches with its *talha dourada* ("gilded woodwork"), as the Holy Sacrament chapel (to the right of the high altar) demonstrates *(see pp8–9).*

2 Santa Clara, Funchal
Founded in 1476 by João Gonçalves de Câmara, son of Zarco *(see p15 & p36)*, this convent has changed little since it was first built *(see pp16–17).*

3 Igreja do Colégio, Funchal
The Jesuits, a brotherhood of missionary priests, owned large wine estates on Madeira, and spent some of their wealth on this lovely church, covered from floor to ceiling in frescoes, gilded carvings and rare ceramic tiles. The school they built alongside is now the University of Madeira. *Praça do Município • Map P3*

Igreja do Colégio, Funchal

4 Igreja do São Pedro, Funchal
The main church until the cathedral was built, St Peter's has a wealth of gilded woodwork, some dating from the 17th century. The corn and grapes being gathered by angels in the right-hand chapel are symbolic of the bread and wine of Christ's Last Supper. A simple slab covers the grave of João de Mourarolim (died 1661), who paid for the decoration. *Rua do São Pedro • Map N2*

5 São Salvador, Santa Cruz
This Gothic parish church was completed in 1512, when the tomb of the merchant Micer João, supported by crouching lions, was installed on the north side. Next to it is the chapel of the Morais family (1522). The altar has 16th-century paintings of the *Life of Christ* by Gregório Lopes, and the sacristy, entered through a Manueline portal, has a 16th-century carved and painted *Last Supper* tableau. *Map K5*

6 Igreja da Nossa Senhora da Conceição, Machico
Probably designed by Pêro Anes, who designed Funchal cathedral, this church dates from 1499 and is noted for its south door – the white marble pillars come from Seville and were a gift from King Manuel I (1495–1521). So, too, was the statue of the Virgin kept in its tabernacle at the peak of the elaborately gilded high altar. *Map K4*

Many churches in Funchal are open from 8am–noon or 1pm, then from 4–7:30pm. Others only open for services (around 8am & 6pm).

7 Capela dos Milagres, Machico

The Chapel of the Miracles takes its name from the 15th-century Flemish crucifix on the high altar. It was miraculously found floating at sea, years after the old chapel was washed away by a flood in 1803. The original chapel is said to have been built over the grave of Anne of Hertford and Robert Machin, legendary lovers shipwrecked here in the 14th century. *Map K4*

8 São Bento, Ribeira Brava

A lion and a basilisk (whose stare was said to turn humans to stone) are among the carvings on the capitals, font and pulpit of this Gothic parish church. Don't miss the magnificent 16th-century Flemish *Nativity* and statue of the Virgin. *Map D5*

Senhora da Luz, Ponta do Sol

9 Senhora da Luz, Ponta do Sol

Founded in 1486 by Rodrigo Anes, one of the first men granted land on Madeira by the Portuguese king, this lovely church has an original knotwork ceiling, a 16th-century Flemish altarpiece, and a unique ceramic font, glazed with green copper oxide to resemble bronze. *Map D5*

10 Capela do Loreto, Loreto

Another unspoiled, historic early church, boasting a knotwork ceiling and Gothic doorways of imported white marble. *Map C4*

Top 10 Religious Figures

1 St Laurence
São Lourenço was the name of the ship in which Captain Zarco *(see p36)* set sail for Madeira in 1420.

2 St Vincent
The patron saint of Portugal and of winemakers is depicted on the ceiling of the church in São Vicente *(see p81)*.

3 Our Lady of Monte
According to local legend, the Virgin gave this statue to a shepherdess *(see p26)*.

4 Our Lady of Terreiro da Luta
This huge statue *(see p78)* was built in thanks for protection during World War I.

5 St Anthony of Padua
The Lisbon-born saint preaches to fish in the Sacred Art Museum *(see p10)* and the Fishermen's Chapel *(see p42)*.

6 St Ignatius Loyola
The founder of the Jesuit order graces the façade of the Colégio *(see p40)*.

7 Christ the Redeemer
Erected in 1927, this clifftop statue *(see p87)* resembles the famous landmark in Brazil's capital, Rio de Janeiro.

8 St Francis and St Clare
Patron saints of Madeira's religious houses, the Santa Clara Convent *(see p16)* and the São Francisco Friary *(see p12)*.

9 Mary Jane Wilson
Indian-born founder of a Madeira-based teaching order. *Wilson Museum: Rua do Carmo 61. Open 10am–noon & 2–5pm Tue–Sat, 10am–noon Sun*

10 Emperor Charles I
Former Austrian emperor, buried in Monte *(see p26)* and beatified by Pope John Paul II.

If you have made a special visit to a church and found it locked, it's worth asking about the key at a nearby store or bar.

Left **Câmara Municipal** Right **House of the Consuls**

TOP 10 Historic Buildings

1 Alfândega, Funchal

Designed in 1508 by Pêro Anes (who also designed the cathedral), the Customs House was built to collect the taxes levied by the Portuguese Crown on Madeira's timber, corn and sugar exports. Now home to the island's Regional Assembly, it has three splendid upper-floor rooms. *Rua da Alfândega • Map P3 • 291 210 500 • By appointment • Free*

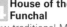

Manueline door, Alfândega (Customs House)

2 Câmara Municipal, Funchal

Madeira's early 19th-century town hall originally belonged to the Count of Carvalhal *(see p24)*. Look in the inner courtyard to see graceful balconies and a sensuous statue of *Leda and the Swan* (1880), brought here when the market was built in 1937 *(see p18)*. *Praça do Município • Map N3 • Ask the porter for permission to view the courtyard*

3 Tower House, Funchal

Opposite the Museum of Sacred Art *(see pp10–11)* is a stately building with a *torre-mirante*. Typical of the grander of Funchal's town houses, these towers were built so the owners could view incoming ships. Note that the door handles are made from large iron keys. *Rua do Bispo • Map P3*

4 House of the Consuls, Funchal

Few traditional Madeiran houses are more ornate than this 18th-century house built for foreign diplomats. *Rua de Conceição • Map P3 • Closed to the public*

5 Fishermen's Chapel, Câmara de Lobos

This simple, moving chapel on the harbour is where fishermen come to pray before and after they put out to sea. Wall paintings depict the story of how St Anthony of Padua (who was born in Lisbon) survived a shipwreck, and was so eloquent that even the fishes of the sea came to hear him preach. *Câmara de Lobos • Map F6*

6 Igreja Inglesa, Funchal

The English Church (1822) is a domed Neo-Classical building set in a delightful garden. Its construction was funded by public appeal; Nelson, George II and the Duke of Wellington all contributed. *Rua do Quebra Costas • Map P2*

7 Capela de Santa Catarina, Funchal

Founded in 1425 by Constança de Almeida, Zarco's wife, this chapel, perched above the harbour, was the first to be built in Funchal. *Jardim de Santa Catarina • Map Q2*

Gold coins paid by the exiled Napoleon for a barrel of Madeira wine are buried beneath the foundation stone of the English Church.

8 Madeira University, Funchal

The 17th-century buildings of this old Jesuit college have been restored to form a new campus. From the inner courtyard, there are good views of the tower of the Igreja do Colégio *(see p40)*.
Rua dos Ferreiros • Map P3

9 Capela do Corpo Santo, Funchal

This 16th-century chapel in the Zona Velha (Old Town) was built and run by the Guild of São Pedro Gonçalves, a self-help charity which raised funds for fishermen and their families. *Rua Dom Carlos I • Map P5*

10 Banco de Portugal, Funchal

The Bank of Portugal building (1940) maintains continuity with traditional architecture, with its globe-topped corner turret, Grecian marble statues, and fruit-filled baskets symbolizing wealth and plenty. Nearby, don't miss Francisco Franco's *Zarco Monument* (1927), showing Funchal's founder looking out to sea.
Avenida Zarco • Map P3

Banco de Portugal

Top 10 Flamboyant Buildings in Funchal

1 The Ritz Restaurant
The former Chamber of Commerce on Avenida Arriaga, now a restaurant, is clad in tile pictures of Madeiran transport.

2 New Chamber of Commerce
Today's Chamber of Commerce is located in a 15th-century building off Rua dos Aranhas.

3 Pátio
The inner courtyard of the 1860s Pátio (Rua da Carreira 43) features a sweeping double staircase leading to the Vicentes Museum *(see p38)*.

4 Rua da Carreira
A street of flamboyant iron balconies – especially at numbers 77–91 and 155.

5 Rua da Mouraria
Funchal's antiques quarter has many aristocratic town houses, including the Museu Municipal *(see p38)*.

6 Garden Gazebo
Take tea, admire the views and watch the world go by at a *casinha de prazer* ("pleasure house") like the one in the Freitas Museum *(see p38)*.

7 Quintas
Ornate mansions like the Quinta Palmeira *(see p45)* line the terraces above Funchal.

9 Casino
The 1970s casino on Avenida do Infante looks wonderful lit up at night.

9 Apartamentos Navio Azul
Reminiscent of an ocean liner, this 1970s block stands beside the Estrada Monumental.

10 Madeira Cable Car Station
This public building is a futuristic cube of steel and glass on Rua Dom Carlos.

Left **Jardim Botânico (Botanical Gardens), Funchal** Right **Quinta do Palheiro Ferreiro**

TOP 10 Gardens

1 Jardim de São Francisco, Funchal

St Francis, the patron saint of the environment, would firmly approve of this richly planted garden, built in the city centre on the site of Funchal's long-gone Franciscan friary. It is only the size of a city block, but so full of scented and flowering plants, shaded by some truly enormous trees, that you could be in the middle of the jungle. ✎ *Avenida Arriaga • Map P2 • Free*

2 Santa Catarina Park, Funchal

On the walk from downtown to the hotel zone, this terraced park has fantastic views over the harbour. Look out for statues of Henry the Navigator at the lower end, Christopher Columbus by the Capela de Santa Catarina *(see p42)* and Francisco Franco's *Semeador* (the "Sower," 1919, *see p39*), symbolically throwing handfuls of seed across the grass. ✎ *Avenida do Infante • Map Q2 • Free*

3 Quinta das Cruzes, Funchal

The flower-filled grounds of this "archaeological park" *(see p14)* boasts grave slabs, a private chapel, a wonderful orchid garden and a *casinha de prazer* ("pleasure house"), perched on the walls to take advantage of the views *(see pp14–15)*.

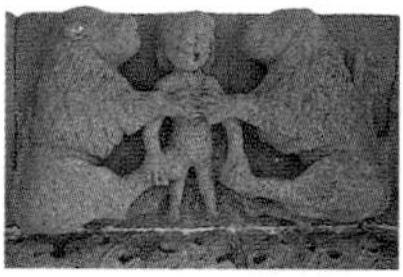

Carved lions in Quinta das Cruzes

Monte Palace Tropical Garden

4 Monte Palace Tropical Garden, Monte

This intriguing botanical garden has caves, fountains, lakes, fish ponds, Japanese temples, sculptures, novel tile pictures and an engaging museum *(see pp28–9)*.

5 Quinta Magnólia, Funchal

The Quinta Magnólia, built in the 1820s as home to the US consul, now houses the Foreign Culture Library. Its palm-filled gardens (with public pool, tennis courts and playground) lie along the terraced flanks of the Ribeira Seca valley. ✎ *Rua do Dr Pita • 9am–dusk Mon–Fri • Map G6 • Free*

6 Quinta Vigia, Funchal

The lovingly maintained official gardens of Madeira's president are open on weekdays, provided that no official functions are taking place. ✎ *Avenida do Infante • Map Q1 • Free*

7 Quinta do Palheiro Ferreiro, Palheiro Ferreiro

Subtropical plants in unusual and imaginative combinations are displayed in a style that is recognizably English *(see pp24–5).*

8 Jardim Botânico, Funchal

These extraordinary gardens are a showcase for Madeira's varied plant life *(see pp20–21).*

9 Hospício Princesa Dona Maria Amélia, Funchal

Popular for wedding photos, this hospital was founded in memory of Brazilian princess Maria Amélia, who died here in 1853.
Avenida do Infante • Map Q1 • Free

10 Quinta Palmeira, Funchal

Despite being blighted by one of Funchal's fast highways, this former home of the Gordon wine family hovers between garden and wilderness, with manicured rose gardens, tiled fountains, grottoes and some jungle-like areas. Don't miss the 15th-century Columbus Window, rescued from the home of João Esmeraldo. *Rua da Levada de Santa Luzia 31A • Map G6 • 291 221 091 • 10am–4pm Tue–Wed (advance booking only) • Adm charge*

Columbus Window, Quinta Palmeira

Top 10 Madeiran Plants and Flowers

1 King Protea
These South African plants, similar to giant artichokes, are in demand for flower displays.

2 Slipper Orchid
Mainly flowering in the winter months, slipper orchids need jungle-like shade.

3 Mexican Poinsettia
These festive plants bloom right on cue for Christmas; note that the showy, scarlet part is actually the bract, not the flower.

4 Aloe
Fleshy leaves edged with spines produce flower spikes up to 1 m (3 ft) high. The sap is harvested, and used in making aloe vera skin products.

5 Agapanthus
The blue-and-white globe-shaped blossoms of the Lily of the Nile line Madeira's roadside banks in summer.

6 Strelitzia
Is it a bird or is it a plant? These long-lived flowers look like exotic birds of paradise.

7 Angel's Trumpet
White, yellow or amber, the datura's long trumpets both smell and look beautiful.

8 Arum Lily
Pure white and sweetly scented, these flowers symbolize the Virgin Mary and virginity.

9 Flame of the Forest
Crowned by orange-red coxcombs, these trees are descended from seed brought to Madeira by Captain Cook in 1772.

10 Jacaranda
Funchal's Avenida Arriaga turns into a river of blue when these striking Brazilian trees flower in spring.

Left **Beach at Praia Formosa** Right **Rock pools, Porto Moniz**

TOP 10 Beaches

1 Praia Formosa

Steep-sided Madeira does not have many beaches – cliffs and rocky shores are the norm – so Praia Formosa ("Beautiful Beach"), a stretch of grey, sea-smoothed pebbles between Funchal and Câmara de Lobos, is a notable exception. Realizing what an assest this could be, the government landscaped the area around the beach and removed the unsightly oil depots. In 2012, the beach was awarded the European Blue Flag for its water quality, environmental management, safety and services. *Map G6*

2 Machico

Positioned near the original basalt pebble beach is the town's artificial alternative, made with sand imported from the Western Sahara in North Africa. The luxuriously soft beach, known as Banda d'Além, is 125 m (410 ft) in length and 70 m (230 ft) wide. It is popular with locals as well as tourists, especially at weekends. *Map K5*

Prainha

3 Ponta do Sol

The beach at Ponta do Sol ("Sun Point") is the perfect place to watch the setting sun. Dramatic clouds float like islands in a pink and purple sky. *Map D5*

4 Jardim do Mar

In October, the narrow strip of west-facing rocky beach connecting Jardim do Mar and Paúl do Mar is the point from which surfers gain access to the waves. Surfers need to bring their own equipment as there are no rental facilities. *Map B4*

5 Porto Moniz

Thundering waves dash Madeira's northern shores along the dramatic north coast road to Porto Moniz, but once there, you can relax in the warm water of natural rock pools. *Map B1*

6 São Jorge

About 2 km (1 mile) east of São Jorge, a sign to *Praia* ("Beach") directs you to the estuary of the São Jorge river, where you can either swim in a natural pool or, in the sea (access is from the small pebbled beach). There's a beach café selling drinks and snacks. *Map H2*

7 Prainha

A pretty, sheltered bay with a beachside café at its eastern end, pocket-sized Prainha ("Little Beach") has one of Madeira's naturally sandy beaches. (Calheta, on the south coast, also has a sandy beach – created with sand imported from Morocco, as does Machico on the east coast). Map L4

8 Garajau and Caniço

A path from the statue of Christ the Redeemer at Garajau winds down to a beach popular for snorkelling and diving. It marks the start of a marine reserve with underwater caves leading to Caniço de Baixo *(see p49)*. Map J6

9 Praia dos Reis Magos

Continuing eastward from Caniço de Baixo, a seafront promenade leads to Praia dos Reis Magos, a rocky beach with a scatter of fishermen's huts and a couple of simple cafés selling freshly grilled fish – idyllic for crowd-shy romantics. Map J6

10 Porto Santo

Travel 40 km (25 miles) north-east of Madeira by a ferry or a flight *(see p103)* to enjoy the vast stretch of unspoilt golden sand of Porto Santo *(see p95)*. One of the two Blue Flag areas of the beach, Fontinha, offers ramps, toilets and amphibian-use wheelchairs for the disabled. Map L2

Long sandy beach, Porto Santo

Top 10 Swimming Pools

1 Royal Savoy Resort

The biggest and best of all the hotel pools *(see p112)*.

2 Reid's

Close competitor to the Savoy, shaded by palms in a garden setting *(see p112)*.

3 Ponta Delgada

This northern town by the coast has two seawater bathing pools and shower facilities. *Map F2*

4 Pestana Porto Santo

This family-friendly all inclusive resort features two huge pools, plus a separate pool for children *(see p112)*. *Map L2*

5 Vidamar Resort Madeira

The hotel has twin infinity pools, a smaller set for kids, and an indoor pool. *Map G6*

6 Ponta Gorda

The adventure pools at this bathing complex are great for kids, while adults can sunbathe overlooking the ocean. *Map G6*

7 Porto Moniz

The collection of rock pools here are famous across the island. Developed to provide a safe, seawater bathing area. *Map C1*

8 Santa Cruz Lido

A mini-Miami; small Art Deco lido with swimming and paddling pools, sea access, and views of landing aircraft. *Map K5 • 10am–6pm daily*

9 Porto da Cruz

Natural rock pools with concrete extensions; enjoy luxuriating in sun-warmed seawater dashed by sea spray. *Map J3*

10 Caniçal

A modern lido with café on the western side of the harbour. *Map L4*

Left **Diving** Right **Golf**

TOP 10 Outdoor Activities

1 Golf

Two of Europe's most scenic courses are located in the east of the island at Santo da Serra and Palheiro Ferreira. Transport can be arranged from Funchal, and equipment hired. *Clube de Golfe de Santo da Serra: Map K4; 291 550 100 • Palheiro Golf: Sítio do Balancal, São Gonçalo; Map J5; 291 790 120*

Canyoning

2 Adventure Sports

Madeira's challenging countryside offers plenty of adventure sports, from trekking and rock-climbing to hang-gliding and orienteering. Companies such as Terras de Aventura and Lokoloko provide organized excursions, and offer all sorts of activities. *291 708 990; www.terrasdeaventura.com • 969 570 780; www.lokolokomadeira.com*

3 Boat Trips

Booths located around Funchal's marina have details of all the cruising options available, from day-long trips to Ilhas Desertas *(see p88)* to shorter sunset cruises. *Funchal Marina • Map Q3 • Madeira Boat Trips: 969 351 568/ 918 375 661 • Bonita da Madeira: 291 762 218*

4 Deep-sea Fishing

Fishing trips can be booked around the marina. A tag-and-release policy ensures fish are released into the wild once caught *(see p106)*. *Funchal Marina • Map Q3 • Turipesca: 291 231 063 • Balancal: 291 790 350 • Nautisantos: 291 231 312*

5 Walking

With more than 1,600 km (994 miles) of rural footpaths to choose from, it's no wonder that thousands of people visit every year just to walk in the island's mountains and forests *(see p50)*.

6 Mountain Biking

The island's rugged terrain presents some challenging tracks, not to mention gravity defying inclines. Following *levada (see pp50–51)* footpaths is an easier option. Rent or join an organized excursion. *Terras de Aventura: 291 708 990; www.terrasdeaventura.com*

7 Birdwatching

The Madeira archipelago offers excellent opportunities for birders. The islands are home to 42 breeding species, three of which are endemic to Madeira: the Zino's petrel, the Trocaz pigeon, and the Madeira firecrest. Seabirds are prevalent, while Berthelot's pipit is a prized sighting. *Madeira Wind Birds: 291 098 007; www.madeira windbirds.com (for expeditions)*

8 Diving

Clean Atlantic waters, clear visibility and an array of beautiful fish and reefs make Madeira a popular spot for divers of all ages and abilities. *Manta Diving Center, Hotel Galomar, Caniço de Baixo; Map J6; 291 935 588 • Madeira Divepoint, Pestana Carlton Madeira Hotel, Largo Antonio Nobre, Funchal; Map H6; 291 239 579*

9 Windsurfing

For the most part fanned by gentle sea breezes, the shallow, crystal-clear water lapping Porto Santo beach *(see p95)* is ideal for windsurfing. Mar Dourado, located on the expansive sands below the Torre Praia Hotel, offers expert windsurfing. Board and equipment hire is also available. The company organizes a range of watersports activities *(see p98)*. *Mar Dourado • 963 970 789 • Map L2*

10 Horse Riding

Several companies in Madeira offer horse riding activities, lessons and guided tours along the island's mountain tracks and forest byways. Similar opportunities also exist on Porto Santo *(see p98)*. *Escapada dos Cavaleiros: Map F5; 291 945 954; www.escapadadoscavaleiros.com • Quinta do Riacho: Map J4; 967 010 015; www.quintadoriacho.com*

Horse riding

Top 10 Madeiran Wildlife

1 Wall Lizards

You will see them on every sunny rock or pavement. They feed on fruit and flies.

2 Wagtails

This yellow-breasted bird is never very far from water, hence its Madeiran nickname: "the washerwoman".

3 Swifts

Watch them wheeling and feeding at dusk along Funchal's seafront promenade.

4 Kestrels

These chestnut-backed birds nest on the cliffs of the hotel district, and hover on the wind in search of prey.

5 Buzzards

Often seen riding the warm air above the valleys of Funchal and Curral das Freiras.

6 Robins

The robins you will see on Madeira have the same cheery red breasts as their mainland cousins, and just as sweet a song.

7 Sally Lightfoot Crabs

These dark brown crabs are often seen grazing tidal rocks for algae. They will disappear fast if threatened – hence "lightfoot".

8 Perez's Frogs

Introduced to Madeira by the Count of Carvalhal, this noisy frog with a bright yellow backbone stripe has spread to every pond in the island.

9 Monarch butterflies

These large orange-black-and-white gliding butterflies are seen in all Madeiran gardens.

10 Limpets

Limpets are a traditional food on Madeira, but harvesting is now controlled to prevent over-exploitation.

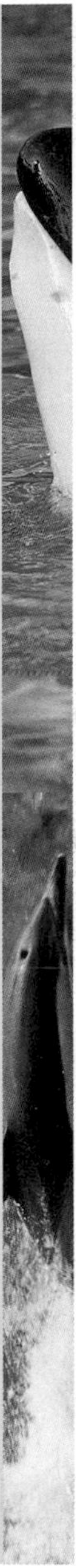

Left **Walkers at Rabaçal** Right **Water feeding a *levada***

TOP 10 Facts about Levada Walking

1 What Are Levadas?

The word *levada* means "to take". A *levada* is an irrigation channel, designed to take water from places where it is plentiful to those where it is not. The Madeirans borrowed the idea from the mountains of Andalucia, where the channels are known as *acequias*.

2 Why Levadas were Built

Water is abundant in the mountains to the north of the island, but scarce in the fertile and sunny south, where most crops are grown. Looking for a way to store water and carry it to their cultivation terraces and fields, the island's early settlers began to build the irrigation channels that form the basis of today's network.

3 Water and Power

Water was essential to the growth of Madeira. It irrigated the wheat, sugar, grape and banana crops, powered the sawmills used to turn trees into timber for construction and ship-building, and turned the wheels of the mills that crushed sugar.

Terracing

4 Levada Maintenance

Levadas require constant maintenance to remove rockfalls and vegetation that could block the flow of water. Paths were constructed alongside the channels to allow the *levadeiro*, or maintenance man, to patrol his length of *levada* and keep it in good working order.

5 Levadas as Footpaths

On a visit to Madeira in 1974, Pat and John Underwood realized that *levada* maintenance paths made perfect footpaths – many of which provide the visitor with easy walking routes, with spectacular views. The resulting guide book, *Landscapes of Madeira* (Sunflower Books), has brought thousands of walkers to the island.

6 Construction

Constructing *levadas* was a feat of engineering. Following the contours meant digging channels into the face of sheer cliffs, or building aqueducts over deep crevices. To reach inaccessible spots, *levada* builders were lowered down cliffs in baskets.

7 Contour Lines

To prevent the water from running too fast, causing soil

erosion, most *levadas* follow the contours of the landscape, winding in and out of valleys, descending gradually from the high peaks of the island's central massif to the ridges and terraces of the south.

8 Guided Tours

Levada walking is easiest if you join a guided tour. Madeira Explorers and Nature Meetings are good companies; the tourist board *(see p102)* will have details of others. *Madeira Explorers: 291 763 701 • Nature Meetings: 291 524 482*

Waterfall, Risco Valley

9 Levada dos Tornos

You can combine a *levada* walk with a visit to the Quinta do Palheiro Ferreiro *(see pp24–5)*. Exit the garden, turn right, and walk up to the village. Beyond the café, look for signs to the Levada dos Tornos and Hortensia Gardens Tea House – an ideal spot for lunch *(see p79)*.

10 Rabaçal

A popular walk, if you are visiting the Paúl da Serra *(see p82)*, starts from Rabaçal. From there, walk down to the Foresters' House, and turn right along the *levada* signposted "Risco". After 20 to 30 minutes' walk through primeval woodland, you will reach a pretty waterfall.

Top 10 Levada Tips

1 Sunflower Guide
Don't go anywhere without an accurate map and reliable directions. Sunflower's *Landscapes of Madeira* has both, and is updated constantly.

2 Dimensions
A typical *levada* is 0.5 m (one and a half ft) wide and 0.8 m (two and a half ft) deep, with narrow paths 1 m (3 ft) wide.

3 How Far Can You Go?
There are now 2,200 km (1,365 miles) of *levada* paths to choose from – it would take three consecutive months to walk them all.

4 Footwear
Paths can be both muddy and slippery, so be sure to wear sensible weatherproof, non-slip footwear.

5 Temperature
It can be cold and wet higher up Madeira's mountains, so take warm and waterproof clothing.

6 Water
Water is everywhere, but it is not fit to drink, so carry your own supplies.

7 Tunnels
Carry a small light so that you can negotiate tunnels without bumping your head.

8 Vertigo
Some *levada* paths have very steep drops. Turn back if you experience dizziness.

9 Last Resort
If vertigo strikes, as a last resort you can always get into the *levada* channel and walk to safety.

10 Vegetation
Levada paths pass trees festooned with hair-like lichen, and cliffs with beautiful and succulent ferns.

A full description of the 30 official footpaths, including levada *routes in Madeira and Porto Santo, can be viewed at www.visitmadeira.pt*

Left **Caves at São Vincente** Right **Parrot Park, Funchal**

Top 10 Children's Attractions

1 Grutas de São Vincente

These caves were created by molten rock. A cave tour, simulated eruptions and a short film will teach you about Madeira's volcanic origins. *São Vicente, Sítio do Pé do Passo • Map E2 • 291 842 404 • Open 10am–6pm daily • Adm charge • www.grutasecentrodovulcanismo.com*

2 Santa Maria de Colombo

There are many boat trips to choose from *(see p48)*, but children will particularly enjoy a trip on a replica of the Santa Maria, the ship that took Columbus across the Atlantic. *Tickets from Marina do Funchal • Map Q3 • 291 220 327 • Trips 10:30am–1:30pm & 3–6pm daily • Adm charge • www.madeirapirateboat.com*

3 Dolphin-watching

Few encounters with nature are as exciting as those with dolphins or whales in their natural habitat, but this trip will appeal more to older children, as a patient wait is not always met with an appearance. *Tickets from Marina do Funchal • Map Q3 • 291 231 312 • Adm charge*

Dolphin-watching

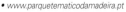

Santa Maria de Colombo

4 Aquaparque

This fabulous landscaped water park features twisting slides, rapids and waterfalls. The Infant Zone's shallow pool and "lazy river" is ideal for toddlers. *Ribeira da Boavista, Santa Cruz • Map K5 • 291 524 412 • Open Jun–Nov: 10am–6pm daily (till 7pm Aug) • Adm charge • www.aquaparque.com*

5 Madeira Theme Park

Set around a boating lake, the park boasts a number of pavilions devoted to the island's heritage and traditions. There's a maze to get lost in and a radical sports zone to check out. Children have their own playground. *Estrada Regional 101, Fonte da Pedra, Santana • Map H2 • 291 570 410 • Open 10am–7pm daily • Closed mid-Jan–mid-Jun: Mon; Sep–mid-Dec • Adm charge • www.parquetematicodamadeira.pt*

6 Santa Catarina Park

Offering a lovely view over the Funchal Bay, these beautiful public gardens *(see p44)* feature a children's playground and a palm-fringed lake where youngsters can feed the resident swans and ducks. *Map Q2*

7 Parrot Park

Depending on the age of your children, you can either let them enjoy the playful antics of parrots and parakeets, or engage them in a discussion about the ethics of keeping wild creatures in cages for human amusement. While you're here, you can also explore the Botanical Garden *(see pp20–21)*.

8 Monte Cable Car

The Monte cable car *(see p27)* flies high over the João Gomes Valley and children under six travel for free. Once in Monte, you can explore the Palace Tropical Garden *(see pp28–9)*. • *Adm charge* • *www.telefericodofunchal.com*

Monte Cable Car

9 Madeira Magic

Recreational and educational, Madeira Magic features 34 interactive exhibits, a mini-planetarium, 3D films and a Magic Garden Tour. *Rua Ponta da Cruz 25, São Martinho • Map G6 • 291 700 708 • Open 10am–6pm Tue–Sun • Adm charge*

10 Living Science Centre

This cultural centre engages young minds with interactive exhibitions. Look out for the 3D film highlighting the UNESCO designated laurissilva forest *(see p23)*. *Rotunda do Ilhéu Mole • Map B1 • 291 850 300 • Open 10am–6pm daily • Adm charge • www.portomoniz.cienciaviva.pt*

Top 10 Tips for Families

1 Hotels

Stay in a five-star hotel for the extra facilities, such as pools, tennis, games rooms, mini-golf and satellite TV.

2 Indulgence

Madeirans love children, so yours will get plenty of friendly attention.

3 Downtown

You can safely let older children wander on their own; crime is almost non-existent.

4 Lido Cinemas

The Forum Madeira Mall *(see p69)* has a multiplex cinema. Foreign films, except animated features, are subtitled. *Map G6 • 291 706 800*

5 History Lesson

Learn about the island at the Madeira Story Centre *(see p39)* that has engaging displays for adults and children.

6 Playgrounds

The best playgrounds in Funchal are in the grounds of Quinta Magnólia and Jardim de Santa Catarina *(see p44)*.

7 Funchal Marina

Stroll around the marina to spot fish, boats and pictures painted on the concrete walls by visiting sailors. *Map Q3*

8 Promenade

Families stroll along Avenida do Mar and buy snacks from Turkish-style kiosks.

9 Porto Moniz

Known as "nature's pools", the rock pools at Port Moniz are great for bathing in warm, shallow water. *Map B1*

10 Porto Santo

Virtually traffic free, Porto Santo is a place to let your children off the leash to explore by bike or on foot.

Left **Madeira Carnival** Right **New Year**

Top 10 Festivals

1 Christmas and New Year
The festive year begins in December when churches and shops mount cribs with a cast of traditional characters, such as rustic shepherds. New Year is even more spectacular. The New Year's Eve fireworks display has been recognized by Guinness Book of Records as the largest in the world.

Flower Festival

2 Carnival
Carnival is celebrated over three days before Shrove Tuesday. Schools, youth clubs and marching bands parade the streets in fancy dress, followed by the colourful allegorical parade that fills the city on the last day. Though not as wild as Rio, this carnival is still an excuse to let your hair down.

3 Flower Festival
Scarcely is Carnival over before the floats come out again for the spring Flower Festival in April/May. Originally created as a tourist attraction, this is a festival that Madeirans have now taken to their heart, with passionate competition among local clubs to produce the best float.

4 Jazz Festival
Staged in Santa Catarina Park *(see p44)*, this prestigious three-day event, held in the first week of July, attracts some of the most famous names in international jazz, such as Jean Luc Ponty and Kenny Garret. Guest musicians include artists from Madeira and mainland Portugal. Jam sessions are staged at selected venues throughout Funchal as an accompaniment to the main programme.

5 Nature Festival
Held in the second week of October, this festival promotes Madeira's natural resources and the best way to experience them either on land, on sea or in the air. The initiative links sports and other outdoor activities with ethnography and Madeiran culture.

6 Columbus Festival
Costumed parades, street theatre, music concerts and exhibitions mark the beginning of September when the residents of Porto Santo's tiny capital, Vila Baleira *(see p95)*, recreate the arrival of Christopher Columbus to the island in the late 15th century.

7 Assumption in Monte
The Virgin is greatly revered by pious Madeirans because they believe she takes pity on human suffering. 15 August, the day on which she is believed to have been assumed into heaven, is observed in Monte *(see p26)*,

For more information on Madeira's festivals, log onto www.visitmadeira.pt

with religious services and processions by day, and feasting, music and dancing by night.

8 Ponta Delgada
Another important religious festival is held in Ponta Delgada *(see p78)* on the first Sunday in September, when pilgrims from all over the island come to pray to the Bom Jesus ("Good Jesus"), a figure of Christ believed to have miraculous powers.

9 Wine Festival
In mid-September, the grape harvest is celebrated in Estreito de Câmara de Lobos, with folk music and demonstrations of grape-crushing done the old-fashioned way – with bare feet. There are also special wine-related menus and events.

10 Atlantic Festival
Held throughout June, the Festival do Atlântico combines fireworks, street entertainment and music festival. There are performances by international stars as well as the accomplished local musicians of the Orquestra Clássica da Madeira, the Orquestra de Mandolins and the Funchal Brass Ensemble.

Atlantic Festival

Top 10 Festive Traditions

1 Street Decorations
When streets are turned into tunnels of flowers, it's a sure sign that a festival is on the way.

2 Festive Greenery
Flower garlands hang from poles wrapped in branches of sweet bay.

3 Flags and Light Bulbs
Bright white bulbs light up the night, and Madeira's flag – a red cross on a white background – is everywhere.

4 Firecrackers
Exploding firecrackers mark the start of a village festival (or a victory by one of the local football teams).

5 Processions and Sermons
Before the fun begins, the serious bit: a religious service to honour the patron saint.

6 Barbecues
No village festival is complete without delicious beef kebabs, barbecued in an old oil barrel.

7 Bolo de Caco
The kebabs are eaten with spongy *bolo de caco* bread, a soft leavened flatbread, baked on top of a stone oven.

8 Wine
Festivals are also a chance to sample local wines (and cider) that are not sold commercially.

9 Wall of Hope
At the Flower Festival, children make a wish and pin posies to a board in front of the town hall.

10 Music and Dance
Brass, accordion and wind bands, known as *filarmónicas*, provide the music for dancing the night away.

Left **Wickerwork demonstration** Right **Boa Vista Orchids**

TOP 10 Specialist Shops

1 O Relógio, Camacha

Packed to the ceiling with furniture, plant pots, baskets and lampshades, there's scarcely room to move in this Aladdin's cave of wicker. If you catch one of the wickerwork demonstrations, you'll see nimble fingers making the bending and weaving of willow canes look much easier than it really is *(see also p89)*. *Largo Conselheiro Aires de Ornelas 12 • Map J5 • 291 922 114 • www.caferelogio.com*

2 Boa Vista Orchids, Funchal

Boa Vista specialize in brightly coloured *bromeliads* ("air plants"), but also grow and sell a great range of other exotic plants. *Rua Lombo da Boa Vista 25 • Map H5 • 291 220 468 • Open 9am–5:30pm Mon–Sat*

3 Jardim Orquídea, Funchal

The Jardim Orquídea aims to convince you that growing orchids is not as difficult as you might think. Visit the laboratory and orchid garden, with its display of 50,000 plants. *Rua Pita da Silva 37 • Map H5 • 915 883 264 • Open 9am–6pm daily • www.madeira-orchid.com*

Orchids

4 Patricio & Gouveia, Funchal

Tour the embroidery factory to learn how traditional designs are transferred from parchment to linen, before browsing the shop for blouses, tableclothes and nightgowns with the beauty of antique lace. *Rua Visconde de Anadia 34 • Map P4 • 291 220 801*

5 Casa do Turista, Funchal

Located in the elegant 19th-century former town house of the German consul, the Tourist house boasts a comprehensive range of Portuguese-made silver, ceramics, glassware and linen. *Rua do Conselheiro José Silvestre Ribeiro 2 • Map Q2 • 291 224 907 • Open 9:30am–6:30pm Mon–Fri, till 1pm Sat*

6 Fado and Folk

The late-night café-music of Portuguese *fado* can become addictive. The best place to find the latest CDs by the superstars of the art – Ana Moura, Mariza, Mísia and Madredeus – is the FNAC music and book store in the Madeira Shopping complex *(see p69)*, which is located on the outskirts of Funchal.

7 Cakes and Pastries

For delicious custard tarts *(pastéis de nata)* for immediate consumption, or *bolo de mel* (honey cake) or *amêndoa torrão* (almond sweetmeats) that will survive the journey home, try Penha d'Águia or A Lua. *Penha d'Águia: Rua das Murças 21. Map P3 • A Lua: Rua da Carreira 78. Map P2*

8 Leather Goods

There are fashionable leather shops aplenty in the narrow streets that lie north and south of Funchal cathedral *(see pp8–9)*, but a factory outlet called Pele Leather has some of the best value leather goods on offer, with an extensive range of leather bags, wallets, clothing, luggage and briefcases to choose from. ⓢ *Rua das Murças 26A, Funchal • Map P3 • 291 223 619*

Bootmaker at Barros e Abreu

9 Barros e Abreu, Funchal

The traditional leather ankle boots made by Barros e Abreu Irmãos are surprisingly comfortable, but unlike their beautiful and timeless leather sandals, they may look out of place back home. See them being made at the workshop in the Zona Velha. Early evening is the best time to drop by. ⓢ *Workshop: Rua do Portão de São Tiago 20–22 • Map Q5*

10 Books

The Livraria Bertrand bookstore at Forum Madeira mall *(see p69)* stocks a useful range of reading material, including maps and books on the history, culture and wildlife of Madeira. Another Funchal bookshop selling most books on Madeira in print is the charmingly old-fashioned Livraria Esperança. ⓢ *Livraria Esperança: Rua dos Ferreiros 119 • Map N3 • 291 221 116*

Top 10 Gifts to Buy

1 Embroidery
Now highly regarded by couturiers, Madeiran embroidery had unlikely beginnings; it was started by Bella Phelps in 1844 to provide work during a slump in the wine trade.

2 Tapestry
Tapestry, a close cousin of embroidery, has been produced on the island since the 1890s. Kits are available for amateur enthusiasts.

3 Wicker
Centred around Camacha, Madeira's wickerworkers create 1,200 different articles.

4 Wine and Liqueurs
As well as fortified Madeira wine, the island produces *poncha*, a potent blend of sugarcane rum, honey and lemon juice.

5 Leather
Leather bags and shoes are a Portuguese speciality.

6 Pottery
Another speciality is pottery in Moorish designs, or shaped like cabbage leaves.

7 Cakes
Festive *bolo de mel* (honey cake), once made only at Christmas, is now a year-round treat, made using cane sugar, nuts and fruit.

8 Flowers
Colourful and long-lasting blooms make a good souvenir of this garden isle.

9 Boots and Sandals
These are handmade in raw leather, to a timeless design.

10 Pompom Hats
Thick, cable-knit hats and sweaters made from raw undyed wool are worn by Madeira's farmers to keep off the chill.

Left **The Old Blandy Wine Lodge** Right **D'Oliveiras**

TOP 10 Wine Outlets

1 The Old Blandy Wine Lodge, Funchal

Set in a former 17th-century friary, this lodge offers wine tastings and tours of its attics. For more in-depth information, take a special Vintage Tour *(see pp12–13)*.

2 Justino's, Funchal

Established in 1870, Justino is one of the island's oldest producers of Madeira wine. Its modern premises stock award-winning labels, including 10-year-old white grape varieties and prized vintages. *Parque Industrial da Cancela, Caniço • Map L4 • 291 934 257 • www.justinosmadeira.com*

3 Vinhos Barbeito, Câmara de Lobos

This revered Madeira wine label ages its wines in giant, iron-hooped barrels of American oak and satinwood. Wines include 3-, 5-, 10- and special 20-year-old bottles and Reserves. *Estrada da Ribeira Gracia, Parque Empresarial de Câmara de Lobos • Map F6 • 291 761 829 • www.vinhosbarbeito.com*

Inspecting for sediment, Vinhos Barbeito

4 Artur de Barros e Sousa, Funchal

Known as ABS, this is one of Madeira's smallest producers; so small that the brothers who run it sell only to "friends" – fortunately, this includes anyone who walks in. *Rua dos Ferreiros 109 • Map N3 • 291 220 622 • Closed Sat, Sun & Aug*

Wine barrels, Artur de Barros e Sousa

5 D'Oliveiras, Funchal

Set in a charming timber barn with a carved stone door that bears the city's coat of arms and the date AD 1619, this wine lodge offers vintages going back to 1850, as well as younger wines, miniatures and gift boxes. *Rua dos Ferreiros 107 • Map N3 • 291 220 784 • Open 9am–6pm Mon–Fri, 9:30am–1pm Sat • www.perolivinhos.pai.pt*

6 Loja dos Vinhos, Funchal

Conveniently located in the heart of the hotel district, and open late for last-minute gift purchases, this wine shop sells the vintages of all of Madeira's main producers, including some rare bottles that date from the 19th century. They will also take telephone orders and make hotel deliveries. *Edifício Eden Mar, Loja 19, Rua do Gorgulho • Map G6 • 291 762 869*

In 1925, The Old Blandy Wine Lodge became the headquarters of the Madeira Wine Company.

7 Henriques & Henriques, Câmara de Lobos

Founded in 1850, this firm has won a string of medals and awards for dispelling the fusty image of Madeira wine and winning back a younger clientele. To this end, they have introduced stylish modern labels and bottle designs, while retaining the traditional qualities of the wines themselves. *Avenida da Altonomia 10 • Map F6 • 291 941 551 • www.henriqueshenriques.pt*

8 Quinta do Furão, Santana

This hotel, restaurant and wine shop belonging to the Madeira Wine Company is set amid extensive vineyards near Santana, in the north of the island. Visitors can follow trails through the vineyards, and help with the harvest during late summer and early autumn (even treading grapes the old-fashioned way). *Achada do Gramacho • Map H2 • 291 570 100 • www.quintadofurao.com*

9 Lagar d'Ajuda, Funchal

This heavily timbered shop set around an antique wine press has a comprehensive stock of ports, sherries and Portuguese regional wines, as well as Madeira from a range of island producers. *Galerias Jardins da Ajuda, Estrada Monumental • Map G6 • 291 771 551*

10 Airport Shop, Madeira Airport

If you suddenly decide you simply cannot go home without a bottle or two of Madeira, the Madeira Wine Company has a duty-free shop at the airport, where you can buy 3-, 5-, 10- and 15-year-old wines, as well as a selection of single-grape, single-harvest vintage wines that are over 20 years old. *Map K5*

Top 10 Madeiran Wine Terms

1 Sercial
The driest of the traditional Madeira wines – excellent as an aperitif or with soup.

2 Verdelho
A tawny, medium dry wine good for drinking with food.

3 Bual/Boal
A nutty dessert wine ideal with cheese or puddings.

4 Malmsey/Malvasia
The richest and sweetest Madeira wine, best for after-dinner drinking.

5 Dry, Medium Dry and Medium Sweet
Wines with these names are three years old, and made from *tinta negra mole* grapes. They lack the depth of real Madeira.

6 Estufagem
The process of ageing the wine in casks kept in an *estufa* (hothouse), or of heating the wine in tanks to make it age even faster. The second method yields inferior results.

7 Canteiro
The term "Canteiro" is used to distinguish quality wines and is a slow method of ageing Madeira in casks heated naturally by the sun.

8 Reserve
A blend of wines made by the two methods of *estufagem* and with an average age of five years. Made mostly with *tinta negra mole* grapes.

9 Special Reserve
A blend of wines aged in casks for about ten years. They are usually made with the noble grape varieties (1–4 above).

10 Vintage Wines
The finest Madeira, aged for a minimum of 20 years in casks and a further two years in the bottle.

For more on Madeira wine See p13

Left **Villa Cipriani** Right **Xôpana at the Choupana Hills Resort**

Top 10 Restaurants

1 Uva, Funchal

Located next to Bar 360°, Uva offers accomplished Mediterranean and Portuguese menus by chef Thomas Faudry and some outstanding top-floor views. *Vine Hotel, Rua dos Aranhas 27 • Map P2 • 291 009 000 • Open 7:30–10:30pm (summer), 6:30–9:30pm (winter) • €€€€*

2 Villa Cipriani, Funchal

Named after the Cipriani Hotel in Venice, this elegant restaurant is owned by Belmond Reid's Palace *(see p112)* and has wonderful sea views and an inventive menu of Italian classics. Dress code: smart casual. *Estrada Monumental • Map H6 • 291 71 71 71 • Open 7–10:30pm • €€€€*

3 Il Gallo d'Oro, Funchal

This Michelin-starred, formal restaurant is renowned for the sophistication of chef Benoît Sinthon's aromatic Mediterranean and Portuguese cuisine. Wine choice is extraordinary. *Cliff Bay Hotel, Estrada Monumental 147 • Map G5 • 291 707 700 • Open 7–10pm • €€€€€*

4 Armada, Funchal

Choose from an à la carte menu or a buffet at Royal Savoy's main restaurant. The tuna steak risotto and duck with ginger are highly recommended. Dress code: smart casual. *Royal Savoy Hotel, Rua Carvalho Araújo • Map H6 • 291 724 238 • €€€€*

5 Quinta da Casa Branca, Funchal

This gourmet restaurant in the 18th-century gate-house of the modern Quinta da Casa Branca hotel *(see p112)* offers dishes such as duck breast in port wine reduction and sweet potato and celery *duo*. Dress code: smart. *Rua da Casa Branca 7 • Map G6 • 291 700 770 • Open 7–10:30pm • €€€€*

6 Chalet Vicente, Funchal

A smart eatery distinguished by its Swiss chalet-style architecture. The menu features kids' portions such as "The Little Lamb". Try the grilled octopus, a Portuguese delicacy. *Estrada Monumental 238 • Map G5 • 291 765 818 • €€€*

Brasserie

7 Brasserie, Funchal

Funchal's smart set have adopted this place, enjoying such dishes as sea bass on olive potato purée. Dress code: smart casual. *Rua Simplício dos Passos Gouveia 29 • Map G6 • 291 763 325 • €€€*

For a guide to restaurant price ranges **See p71**

8 Casa Velha do Palheiro, São Gonçalo

The seven-course gourmet menu at this former hunting lodge, built in 1804 by the Count of Carvalhal, gathers inspiration from far and wide. Roast pigeon "Apicius" owes its origins to the ancient Roman cookery writer; gin-and-tonic sorbet is a witty reference to the country-house lifestyle; salad of fresh scallops and *foie gras* is delicious. Dress code: smart casual. *Rua da Estalagem 23 • Map H6 • 291 790 350 • Closed L daily • €€€€€*

Casa Velha do Palheiro

9 Xôpana at the Choupana Hills Resort, Funchal

Designed by Didier Lefort, the Xôpana is a feast for the eyes as well as the taste buds. Casual diners can enjoy a perfect beef-burger, while gourmets can choose creative dishes. Dress code: smart casual. *Travessa do Largo da Choupana • Map H5 • 291 206 020 • €€€€*

10 A Morgadinha, Funchal

Tangy Goan dishes such as *dampak* (beef with yoghurt sauce, coriander and sweet spice) typify the authentic menu at this boutique hotel restaurant. The selection of regional and international dishes is also delicious. *Estalagem Quintinha de São João, Rua de Levada de São João 4 • Map H5 • 291 740 920 • €€€€*

Top 10 Madeiran Dishes

1 Sopa de Tomate e Cebola
Tomato and onion soup crowned with a boiled egg and garnished with chopped parsley.

2 Açorda
Soup flavoured with garlic and coriander, made with bread and golden olive oil, topped off with a poached egg.

3 Espetada
Herb-flavoured barbecued beef, sometimes served on skewers that hang from a frame by your table.

4 Milho Frito
Deep-fried maize (like Italian polenta), traditionally served with *espetada*, though fries are now more common.

5 Lapas
Limpets, plucked from Madeira's rocky shores and grilled with garlic butter.

6 Bolo de Caco
Madeiran leavened flat-bread, baked on top of the oven and served plain or with garlic and herb butter.

7 Espada
Scabbard fish, a succulent and (usually) boneless white fish, traditionally served grilled with fried banana.

8 Prego
Delicious Madeiran fast food – grilled steak in a bread bun (*prego special* has ham and/or cheese as well).

9 Picado
Succulent pieces of beef, fried with garlic and red peppers, served with French fries.

10 Bacalhau
Dried salted cod – very traditional, but an acquired taste, served in many ways including with potatoes and egg, or casseroled with tomatoes and onion.

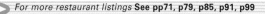

For more restaurant listings **See pp71, p79, p85, p91, p99**

AROUND MADEIRA

Left **Funchal University courtyard** Right **Fortaleza de São Tiago**

Funchal

FOUNDED IN 1425, FUNCHAL WAS GRANTED CITY STATUS IN 1508. *Despite being over 500 years old, many of its finest historical buildings are still intact, despite fire, piracy and earthquake. Named Funchal ("fennel") because of the wild fennel plants found growing in abundance by the first settlers, Madeira's capital sits on the island's southern coast in a natural amphitheatre, hemmed in by cliffs to the east and west, and steep green mountains to the north. Its streets are paved with black-and-white mosaics, and lined by blue-flowered jacaranda trees. Numerous public parks and private gardens make this a festive city of heady scents and colours, where architecture and nature are delightfully combined.*

Top 10 Sights

1. Zona Velha
2. Carmo Quarter
3. Cathedral Quarter
4. Around the Town Hall
5. University Quarter
6. Around Avenida Arriaga
7. Rua da Carreira
8. São Pedro and Santa Clara
9. Hotel Zone
10. Seafront and Marina

View across Funchal to the mountains beyond

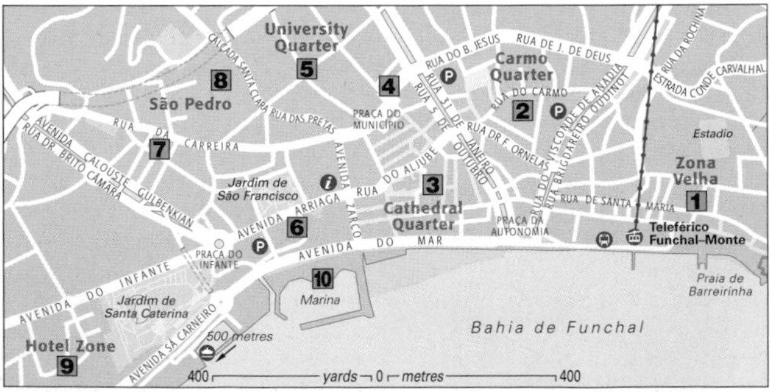

Preceding pages **Funchal's Câmara Municipal (Town Hall), set at the eastern end of the Praça do Município**

Rua Santa Maria, Zona Velha

1 Zona Velha

Funchal was the first city since Roman times to be built by Europeans outside of Europe, and the Zona Velha (Old Town) is where it began. The original settlement was protected by the Fortaleza de São Tiago, now the Museum of Contemporary Art *(see p68)*. Today, restaurants and bars line the rejuvenated Rua de Santa Maria and cluster around the Capela do Corpo Santo *(see p43)*. A seafront promenade and park link the Old Town to the Monte cable car station *(see p53)* and the covered market *(see pp18–19)*. Here, you will also find the Madeira Story Centre *(see p39)*. ✎ *Map P5*

2 Carmo Quarter

The Carmo Quarter lies between two of the three rivers that flow from mountain to sea through Funchal. As they pass through the city, their deep channels are overhung with purple and red bougainvillea. Linking the 17th-century Carmo Church, the Franco Museum *(see p39)* and IBTAM is a warren of narrow streets, with fine buildings like the House of the Consuls *(see p42)*. ✎ *Map N4*

***Leda and the Swan,* outside Town Hall**

3 Cathedral Quarter

When Christopher Columbus came to stay with his friend João Esmeraldo in 1498, the cathedral *(see pp8–9)* and the Alfândega (Customs House) *(see p42)* were still being built. Esmeraldo's home was later transformed into the now closed City of Sugar Museum, and the Customs House, a short step away from the sociable pavement cafés surrounding the cathedral, has become Madeira's regional parliament building. ✎ *Map P3*

4 Around the Town Hall

Chic clothing shops line the narrow pedestrian streets that stretch up in a grid from the cathedral to the city's one and only open square, with its fountain, its flower sellers, and its fish-scale-patterned paving. Framing the square is the graceful Baroque Câmara Municipal (Town Hall) *(see p42)* and the pretty, arcaded Bishop's Palace, now the Museu de Arte Sacra (Museum of Sacred Art) *(see pp10–11)*. ✎ *Map P3*

5 University Quarter

Animated saints dance and gesticulate from niches in the façade of the marvellous Igreja do Colégio *(see p40)*, the huge and ornately decorated Jesuit church whose ancient school buildings have been restored to form the main campus of Madeira University *(see p43)*. Exploring the six city blocks to the north and on either side of the campus, you will find old-fashioned bookshops, cobbled wine lodges *(see p58)*, and some of Funchal's oldest and most ornate tower houses. ✎ *Map N2*

São Pedro Church

6 Around Avenida Arriaga

Wide and leafy Avenida Arriaga is lined with some of Funchal's most prestigious public buildings. They include the offices of the regional government, the imposing Bank of Portugal building *(see p43)*, the Old Blandy Wine Lodge *(see pp12–13)*, the tourist office and its next-door art gallery, and the flower-filled São Francisco Gardens on the north side. On the south side is the huge São Lourenço fortress with its battlemented walls *(see p68)*,

Detail of Fortaleza de São Tiago

the Ritz Restaurant with its tiled exterior *(see p43)*, the theatre *(see p70)* and its chic café, and several good shopping arcades *(see p69)*. ◈ *Map P2*

7 Rua da Carreira

A stroll down Rua da Carreira reminds you why Funchal was once known as "Little Lisbon". The elegant buildings of this bustling street, with their green shutters and ornamental iron balconies hung with plants, are a taste of the Portuguese capital. At No. 43, the Vicentes Museum *(see p38)*, with its *belle époque* staircase, sets the theme. At the western end, a pretty *casa de prazer* (garden gazebo) sits on the corner of Rua do Quebra Costas, the street that leads to the secluded gardens of the Igreja Inglesa (English Church) *(see p42)*. ◈ *Map P2*

8 São Pedro and Santa Clara

The streets north of Rua da Carreira have some of Funchal's best museums. The Museu Municipal *(see p38)* in Rua Mouraria has a pretty herb garden next to it, and the church of São Pedro *(see p40)* is lined with 17th-century tiles. The steep Calçada de Santa Clara leads to the Freitas Museum *(see p38)*, Santa Clara Convent *(see pp16–17)* and the Quinta das Cruzes Museum *(see pp14–15)*. If you have energy left, keep on up to the Fortaleza do Pico ("Peak Fortress") *(see p68)* for panoramic views. ◈ *Map N2*

Calçada Pavements

The pavements and squares of Funchal are works of art. Blocks of dove-grey basalt and creamy limestone are laid in mosaic patterns of great intricacy and beauty, from the fish-scale pattern of the Town Hall square to the heraldic patterns and floral motifs along Avenida Arriaga. There are even complete pictures along Rua João Tavira, north of the cathedral, depicting the city's coat of arms, a wine carrier and the ship that brought Zarco *(see p15)* to Madeira.

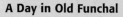

9 **Hotel Zone**

West of the city, you can stroll through a succession of parks *(see p44)* and enjoy the varied architecture of the Art Deco mansions from the 1920s and 1930s lining the Avenida do Infante. As the road crosses the ravine of the Ribeira Seco ("Dry River") and curves past Belmond Reid's Palace, the island's most prestigious hotel *(see p112)*, mansions give way to big hotels which march along the clifftops, interspersed with shopping centres and restaurants. *Map Q1*

10 **Seafront and Marina**

Everything in Funchal looks out to the sparkling sea and bustling harbour, where private yachts, container ships and cruise liners on transatlantic voyages call in. A programme of redevelopment is set to modernize the port and marina, which were damaged by floods in 2010 *(see p37)*. Stroll along Avenida do Mar to soak up the sunshine, and sample coffee and cakes at the onion-domed kiosks along the seafront. *Map Q3*

Funchal Marina

A Day in Old Funchal

Morning

A visit to the **cathedral** will introduce you to the two main styles of Madeiran church architecture: 16th-century Gothic and 18th-century Baroque.

Walk three blocks north to the **Sacred Art Museum**, where the island's finest works of art demonstrate how rich Madeira became when it was Europe's main source of sugar.

Enjoy Funchal's laid-back café life in one of the pavement cafés on **Praça do Município.**

Follow Rua C Pestana and Rua da Carreira westward out of the square to enjoy the lace-like balconies that decorate the upper storeys; allow half an hour to see the ceramic tile collection at the **Freitas Museum** (open 10am–5:30pm Tue–Sat).

Afternoon

Take your pick of the restaurants along **Rua da Carreira** for a leisurely lunch, or head in the direction of the market and explore the **Zona Velha**.

Returning to Calçada de Santa Clara around 2pm, visit the shady gardens and art-filled rooms of the **Quinta das Cruzes**; then take a guided tour of **Santa Clara Convent**.

Wind down after a day of culture by taking the 4:30pm tour of the Old Blandy Wine Lodge – the oldest on Madeira.

Finish the day with a stroll along Avenida do Mar, or enjoy the harbour view from **Santa Catarina Park**.

Funchal is best explored between Tuesday and Friday. Churches and museums are closed during lunch, but shops and cafés stay open.

Left **Cemitério Britânico**

Top 10 Best of the Rest

1 Museu de Arte Contemporânea
The 17th-century Fortaleza de São Tiago makes a superb setting for late 20th-century works of art. *Rua do Portão de São Tiago • Map Q6 • 291 213 340 • 10am–12:30pm & 2–5:30pm Mon–Sat • Adm charge*

2 Museu de Electricidade "Casa da Luz"
This former power station shows what heroic efforts were needed to bring electricity to the island. *Rua da Casa da Luz 2 • Map P4 • 291 211 480 • 10am–12:30pm & 2–6pm Tue–Sat • Adm charge*

3 Núcleo Museológico do Bordado
The history of embroidery, tapestry and handicrafts on Madeira, with an introduction to the island's colourful costumes. *Rua do Visconde do Anadia 44 • Map N4 • 291 211 600 • www.bordadomadeira.pt • 9:30am–12:30pm & 2–5:30pm Mon–Fri • Adm charge*

4 Art Opens Doors
This project sees the doors in Madeira's oldest street. Striking designs by local and international artists are on display. *Rua de Santa Maria (Old Town) • Map P4-5 • www.arteportasabertas.com • Free*

5 Palácio de São Lourenço
The historic fortress has displays on the pirate Bertrand de Montluc *(see p31)*. *Avenida Zarco • Map P3 • 291 202 530 • Guided tours 12:30pm Mon, 10am Tue–Wed, 10am & 12:30pm Thu, 3pm Fri • Free*

6 Cemitério Britânico
Protestants of all nations are buried in this garden-like cemetery whose ancient headstones tell many a poignant story. *Rua da Carreira 235 • Map P1 • 8am–5pm Mon–Fri (ring bell at gate) • Free*

7 Fortaleza do Pico
The stiff uphill walk to the 17th-century Peak Fortress is rewarded by sweeping views and a one-room museum on the history of Funchal's defences. *Rua do Forte • Map N1 • 9am–6pm daily • Free*

8 Lido Promenade
A seafront promenade follows the clifftops west of the city from the Lido to Praia Formosa, with landscaped gardens and ever-changing views. *Rua Gorgulho • Map G6*

9 Museu do Brinquedo
From 19th-century china dolls to 1980s plastic Barbies, over 100 years of toy history, with a huge collection of miniature cars. There is a ground-floor restaurant. *Rua da Levada dos Barreiros 48 • Map G6 • 919 922 722 • 10am–8pm Tue–Sat, 11am–6pm Sun • Adm charge*

10 Universo de Memórias
A thought-provoking exhibition of memorabilia collected by traveller, writer, politician and artist João Carlos Abreu, on his trips to different countries. *Santa Clara Civic and Cultural Centre, Calçada do Pico 2 • Map N1 • 291 225 122 • 10am–5pm Tue–Sat • Adm charge*

Left **Cabbage leaf plate, Casa do Turista** Right **Embroidery at Bazar Oliveiras**

Top 10 Places to Shop

1 Mercado dos Lavradores
Make it a daily habit while in Funchal to visit the market and shop for picnic ingredients or souvenirs, or simply savour the colourful bustle *(see pp18–19)*.

2 Madeira Shopping
Providing retail therapy for serious shopaholics, this huge mall features top brands in over 100 stores. Follow signs from the São Martinho exit of the Via Rapida, or take the Horários do Funchal bus 8 from the city centre. ✎ *Caminho de Santa Quitéria 45, Santo António • Map G5*

3 Casa do Turista
All the elegance of a bygone era: Madeiran and mainland Portuguese textiles, ceramics, silver and glassware displayed in a stately town house *(see p56)*.

4 Galerias São Lourenço
At Funchal's most upmarket shopping mall, you will find everything from sunglasses and children's clothes to elegant kitchen- and tableware. ✎ *Avenida Arriaga 41 • Map P2*

5 Arcadas de São Francisco
The cobbled yard where wine barrels were once made for The Old Blandy Wine Lodge *(see pp12–13)* is now an upscale mall dedicated to selling fashionable apparel, jewellery and furnishings. ✎ *Rua de São Francisco 20 • Map P2*

6 Dolce Vita Shopping
This modern temple to consumerism boasts eye-catching architecture and a city centre location. It houses a plethora of fashion boutiques, jewellers, leisurewear and sports shops, as well as a hypermarket. ✎ *Rua Dr Brito Câmara 9 • Map P1*

7 Rua das Murças
Come to this narrow city-centre street for keenly priced shops like Bazar Oliveiras (No. 6), selling leather, embroidery, tapestry, and all kinds of Madeiran souvenirs. Most shops open 10am–8pm daily. ✎ *Map P3*

8 Antiques Quarter
Shops selling contemporary art or old maps and engravings, chests, chandeliers, mirrors and Chinese spice jars, furniture and clocks. ✎ *Rua da Mouraria and Rua de São Pedro • Map P2, N2*

9 Forum Madeira
This stylish mall houses over 80 stores, a giant hypermarket, 17 restaurants and six cinemas. Sea views can be enjoyed from the rooftop terrace. ✎ *Estrada Monumental 390, Lido • Map G6*

10 Rua Dr. Fernão Ornelas
Funchal's main shopping street is a wonderful mix of chic boutiques sitting cheek-by-jowl with grocers selling coffee and pungent salt cod. Most shops close on Saturday afternoon and Sunday. ✎ *Map P4*

Left **Casino da Madeira** Right **Teatro Municipal**

TOP 10 Nights Out

1 Venda Velha
Madeira's potent tipple, *poncha (see p57)*, is served with gusto at this bar. On Friday and Saturday nights, the revelry spills out on to the cobbled terrace. ◎ *Rua de Santa Maria 170 • Map Q6 • 925 003 460 • Open noon–4am daily; winter hours may vary*

2 Teatro Municipal
The resplendent theatre (built 1888) hosts music recitals, contemporary dance, drama (usually in Portuguese) and art-house movies. Look for billboards outside the theatre. ◎ *Avenida Arriaga • Map P2 • 291 215 130*

3 Café do Teatro
The romantic night-time haunt of Funchal's smart set, this small but sophisticated café offers cocktails, chat and occasional DJs. ◎ *Avenida Arriaga 40 • Map P2 • 291 226 371*

4 Casino da Madeira
Play slot machines, roulette and blackjack at this casino, or enjoy the spectacular dinner shows and live music in the Copacabana Bar. ◎ *Avenida do Infante (in the grounds of the Pestana Casino Park Hotel) • Map H6 • 291 140 424 • Open 3pm–3am Sun–Thu, 4pm–4am Fri, Sat and bank holidays*

5 Scat Funchal Jazz Club
Enjoy live jazz concerts by national and international performers at this bar/restaurant. ◎ *Promenade do Lido • Map G6 • 291 765 500 • www.scatfunchalmusicclub.com*

6 Discoteca Vespas
Three clubs under the same roof cater to a youthful clientele. ◎ *Avenida Sá Carneiro 7 (opposite the container port) • Map Q2 • 291 234 800*

7 23 Vintage
Tucked away in Funchal's old town, this fashionable late-night bar is a popular local hang-out. The music evokes the spirit of the 1970s, 80s and 90s. ◎ *Rua de Santa Maria 27 • Map Q6 • 291 630 339 • Open 8pm–2am*

8 Sabor a Fado
Enjoy live music by the waiting staff at this pleasant restaurant. It offers an authentic and traditional Portuguese menu. ◎ *Travessa das Torres 10 • Map P5 • 925 612 259*

9 Folk Music and Dance
Madeira's *charamba* was sung to ease the daily grind. Roving bands of musicians and dancers visit the Marina Terrace on Avenida do Mar most evenings. You can even book a show at the Cliff Bay Resort Hotel. ◎ *Cliff Bay: Estrada Monumental 147 • Map G6 • 291 707 707*

10 Classical Concerts
The Mandolin Orchestra plays at the English Church on Friday nights (except in August). For Madeira's Orquestra Clássica and the Brass Ensemble, see posters on Avenida Arriaga. ◎ *English Church: Rua Quebra Costas 18 • Map P1 • 291 220 674 • www.orquestradebandolinsdamadeira.net*

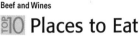

Beef and Wines

Price Categories

For a three course meal for one with half a bottle of wine (or equivalent meal), taxes and extra charges.

€	under €15
€€	€15–€25
€€€	€25–€40
€€€€	€40–€60
€€€€€	over €60

TOP 10 Places to Eat

1 Zarco's
It's worth the short taxi ride to sit on a terrace with a classic westerly view of Funchal Harbour while dining on classic Madeiran *espetadas* of beef, chicken and fish from the open grill. *Estrada Conde Carvalhal 136A, São Gonçalo • Map H6 • 291 795 599 • €€*

2 Arsénio's
Listen to live *fado* (traditional Portuguese café music) every night at 8pm while dining on succulent kebabs in the Zona Velha (Old Town). *Rua da Santa Maria 169 • Map P5 • 291 224 007 • €€€*

3 Riso Risottoria del Mundo
Offering pleasant ocean views, this eatery is all about rice, from paella to risotto. The green asparagus risotto with grilled scallops and hazelnut pesto is typical of the menu. *Rua de Santa Maria 274 • Map Q6 • 291 280 360 • Closed Mon • €€€*

4 Restaurante do Forte
Upmarket but informal, this romantic restaurant, set within the walls of the 17th-century São Tiago fort, serves excellent Portuguese cuisine, with set menus offering great value. *Rua Portão São Tiago • Map Q6 • 291 215 580 • €€€€*

5 Tasca Literaria Dona Joana-Rabo-de-Peixe
Try the *Guacamole à "Remelico"* with a glass of red wine at this quirky tapas bar. *Rua de Santa Maria 77 • Map P5 • 291 220 348 • Open 11am–midnight Sun–Thu, till 2pm Fri–Sat • €€*

6 Beef and Wines
Brazilian specialities such as *picanha* (grilled rump of beef) and *feijoada* (black-bean stew). Some fish and seafood; local scabbard fish is served with a passion fruit sauce. Wine list features over 200 labels. *Edificio Infante Dom Henrique 206, Avenida do Infante • Map H6 • 291 282 257 • Open noon–midnight daily • €€€*

7 Taj Mahal good
Try tandoori king prawn, fish tikka massala and *kulfi* ice cream at this stylish Indian restaurant set in a glass conservatory near the Carlton Madeira Hotel. *Rua Imperatriz Dona Amélia 119 • Map H6 • 291 228 038 • €€€*

Also 'Red Lion' - v.good

8 Doca do Cavacas
This rustic beachside bar is renowned for freshly caught fish served to the sound of crashing waves. *Rua Ponta da Cruz (western end of Estrada Monumental) • Map G6 • 291 762 057 • Closed Mon • €€€*

9 O Barqueiro
Arguably the best and most varied fish restaurant on Madeira. If you're spoilt for choice, try the "tasting menu", but avoid the over-priced lobster. *Rua Ponta da Cruz (western end of Estrada Monumental) • Map G6 • 291 761 229 • €€€*

10 Dona Amélia
This fine dining restaurant serves classic regional and Mediterranean specialities. Booking is advisable. *Rua Imperatriz D Amélia 83 • Map Q1 • 291 225 784 • €€€€*

Quinta do Palheiro Ferreiro (Blandy's Gardens)

Central Madeira

CENTRAL MADEIRA CONSISTS ALMOST ENTIRELY *of high volcanic peaks and deep ravines. To experience this scenic grandeur to the full, you really do have to walk, but thanks to some well-placed* miradouros *(scenic viewing points), you can come away with some memorable photographs and gain a sense of the immense visual appeal of the central mountain range even when travelling by road. Between the north and the south, there are great contrasts. Soaked in sunshine, the southern slopes are densely populated, with red-tiled farmhouses lost in a sea of vines and bananas. The northern slopes are densely wooded; along the coastal strip, tiny terraces cling to the steep valley sides making a colourful patchwork of many different hues of green.*

Câmara de Lobos

Top 10 Sights

1. Monte
2. Quinta do Palheiro Ferreiro
3. Jardim Botânico
4. Câmara de Lobos
5. Cabo Girão
6. Curral das Freiras
7. Pico do Arieiro
8. Ribeiro Frio
9. Santana
10. Pico Ruivo

Preceding pages **Step-like terraces cut into a hillside near São Vicente, Western Madeira**

Monte cable car

1 Monte

Take the cable car from Funchal's Zona Velha up to Monte, and you will sail 600 m (1,968 ft) up the southern face of Madeira to a place that seems more garden than village, shaded by veteran trees and watered by natural springs *(see pp26–7)*.

2 Quinta do Palheiro Ferreiro

Thanks to a period spent in exile in England during the early 19th century, the first owner of this estate, the Count of Carvalhal, developed a love of meadows, woods and streams, and laid the foundations for today's richly varied garden *(see pp24–5)*.

3 Jardim Botânico

Come here to satisfy your curiosity about the names and origins of all the flowering trees, palms, succulents and scented climbers that grow everywhere in Madeira – in front gardens, in public parks and along country roads *(see pp20–21)*.

4 Câmara de Lobos

The *lobos* ("wolves") in the name of this pretty village refer to the monk seals that once basked on the pebbly beach. This is now used as an open-air boatyard, where traditional craft are repaired or given a fresh coat of blue, red and yellow paint, laid on in bold stripes. Down among the noisy bars is the Fishermen's Chapel, where villagers give thanks for the safe return of their men after a long night at sea, fishing for *espada* (scabbard fish), most of which ends up on the tables of Madeira's many restaurants. *Map F6 • All Rodoeste buses call here*

5 Cabo Girão

Madeira's highest sea cliff, 580m (1,903 ft) above the ocean, also claims to be the second highest in the world, although opinions in fact differ over whether the highest is in Norway, the Orkneys or Ireland. From the viewing point perched on the summit, you gaze down to a *fajã*, a rock platform created when part of the cliff face fell into the sea millennia ago. Local farmers cultivate crops here in neat terraces. If you want a closer look, you can take the cable car *(teleférico)* from Caldeira Rancho, on the western side of Câmara de Lobos, down to the base of the cliff. *Map E5 • Rodoeste bus 154*

Jardim Botânico (Botanical Gardens)

View of Curral das Freiras

6 Curral das Freiras

A long road-tunnel now links the valley village of Curral das Freiras with the wider world, the old road having been closed due to safety concerns. Upon arrival in "Nun's Refuge", you will gain a sense of just how isolated this community once was *(see pp30–31)*.

7 Pico do Arieiro

In the colourful landscape of Madeira's third highest peak, you can read the story of the volcanic forces that created the island, and the elemental battles between wind, rock and rain that eroded it into jagged peaks and plunging ravines *(see pp32–3)*.

A-framed Houses

The colourful A-framed houses of the Santana district were probably introduced by early settlers from the farming districts of central Portugal. Today, they are used as houses, or as cattle byres. On an island of precipitous slopes, cattle can easily fall if left to graze freely, so they are kept in the cool shade of the thatched *palheiros*, to which their owners carry stacks of freshly cut grass and foliage at intervals during the day.

8 Ribeiro Frio

The "Cold River" of this valley clearing tumbles down the mountainside to bring clear water to a trout farm set in a pretty garden planted with Madeira's native flowers. Some of the trout inevitably end up on the menu of the Restaurante Ribeiro Frio opposite, a good place to begin or end a short walk along the dry *levada* to Balcões. A longer walk to Portela starts just below the restaurant; you need a map and guidebook to do the whole route, but you can enjoy splendid views of the dense green forest by sampling the first stretch. *Map H4 • Carros de São Gonçalo bus 103*

9 Santana

Santana has Madeira's best examples of the traditional

A-framed houses, Santana

The weather on Pico do Arieiro is often clearest in the first part of the morning and in the evening, so plan your walk accordingly.

timber-and-thatch dwellings known as *palheiros*. These brightly-painted triangular houses are comfortable but compact, and many now have modern extensions to accommodate the kitchens and bathrooms that the originals lacked. You can visit and take photographs of a row of tourist-board houses next to the church, but wander the lanes of the village and you will see plenty more, with immaculate gardens. *Map H2 • Carros de São Gonçalo bus 103*

View from Pico Ruivo

10 Pico Ruivo

Madeira's highest peak is reached from the road next to the petrol station on the eastern side of Santana. This leads to the car park at Achada do Teixeira, from where a well-paved path climbs to the summit (1,862 m, 6,109 ft). To the south, the views look over the high peaks and jagged ridges of an arid volcanic landscape; to the north, clouds hang around the lush, forested slopes. Back at the car park, look for the eroded rocks called Homem em Pé ("Standing Man") in a hollow behind the rest house. *Map G3 • No bus*

A Day in Central Madeira

Morning

Starting in **Monte** by 10am at the latest, your first stop is the summit of **Pico do Arieiro**. (If it's too cloudy, do the trip in reverse; the weather may clear later on.)

Afterward, descend to **Ribeiro Frio** to visit the trout farm and enjoy the native Madeiran flowers in the surrounding gardens.

Walk downhill past the shop, and take the *levada* path signposted left to **Balcões**. A 20-minute stroll through woodland brings you to a cutting in the rock with wonderful views over the island's central peaks and valleys.

For lunch, try the small café at Ribeiro Frio. If you prefer to bring your own food, there are picnic areas in the vicinity. Alternatively, continue on to **Santana.**

Afternoon

If you're not already in Santana, make your way there; the main attractions are the traditional triangular houses and the **Madeira Theme Park** *(see p52)*. Next, follow signs to the Rocha do Navio Teleférico, and you will find a cable car and footpath to **Santana's beach**.

Now head west into **Faial**. Two "balconies" along the way give you memorable views of **Penha de Águia** ("Eagle Rock"). In Faial itself, there are numerous signposted walks.

If you're staying in Fuchal, the fastest route back is to follow signs to Machico through a long tunnel that links up at the southern end with the airport road back to the city.

Old sugar mill, Porto da Cruz

TOP 10 Best of the Rest

1 Terreiro da Luta
Pious Madeirans believe that the Virgin appeared to a young shepherd girl on this spot and gave her the statue now in Monte church. The present memorial was erected after German U-boats attacked ships in Funchal Harbour in 1916; the Virgin's help was sought and the bombardment stopped. *Map H5*

2 Queimadas
From western Santana, a road signposted to "Queimadas" gives way to a track leading to a house with gardens, ponds and picnic tables deep in the green-wooded heart of the UNESCO World Natural Heritage forest. *Map H3*

3 Caldeirão Verde
From Queimadas, take a scenic *levada* walk to the "Green Cauldron", a waterfall cascading down a rock hollow. Sturdy footwear, torches (flashlights) and waterproofs essential. *Map G3*

4 Ponta Delgada
At Ponta Delgada's church, see the miraculous statue, found floating at sea in the 16th century. When the church burned down in 1908, it was found charred but intact in the embers. *Map F2*

5 Boaventura
Boaventura makes a great base for exploring the orchards watered by the Levada de Cima. Make sure to take a good walking guide *(see p50)*. *Map G2*

6 São Jorge
São Jorge has a Baroque church from 1761. A 19th-century lighthouse sits on Ponta de São Jorge, with views of the coast. A side road east of the village leads to a small, sheltered beach *(see p46)*. *Map H2*

7 Faial
The Fortím do Faial is a toy-town fort built in the 18th century to fend off pirates. South of the village are views of Penha de Águia and the newly formed rock platform *(fajã)*, where part of the cliff fell into the sea. *Map J3*

8 Penha de Águia
"Eagle Rock" rises 590 m (180 ft) from the sea, casting its shadow over neighbouring villages. Young Madeirans regard the climb from Penha de Águia de Baixo to the top as a test of strength and endurance. *Map J3*

9 São Roque de Faial
Several valleys meet at São Roque, so walkers can start at the church and choose one of the paths that go west up the Ribeiro Frio ("Cold River") or east up the Tem-te Não Caias (literally, "Hold on; don't fall"). *Map J3*

10 Porto da Cruz
The Old Town is a maze of cobbled alleys. A sugar mill stands by the harbour, where visitors can buy the locally distilled spirit *aguardente*. *Map J3*

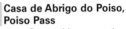

Casa de Abrigo do Poiso

Price Categories

For a three course meal for one with half a bottle of wine (or equivalent meal), taxes and extra charges.	
€	under €15
€€	€15–€25
€€€	€25–€40
€€€€	€40–€60
€€€€€	over €60

Top 10 Places to Eat

1 Adega da Quinta, Estreito de Câmara de Lobos
Rustic Madeiran cuisine is the speciality at this hotel restaurant. Try the succulent *espetada* (meat kebab), roasted in a wood-burning oven. Impeccable service. *Quinta do Estreito, Rua José Joaquim da Costa • Map F5 • 291 910 530 • €€€*

2 Hortensia Gardens Tea House, São Gonçalo
West of the the Levada dos Tornos, the homely Hortensia serves scones, pies and cakes. *Caminho dos Pretos 89 • Map H6 • 291 795 219 • Open 10am–6pm • €*

3 Churrascaria O Lagar, Câmara de Lobos
This big, pink palace in the hills overlooking the town serves perfectly tender garlic-flavoured chicken and skewers of beef, with warm rounds of cake-like *bolo de caco* bread, liberally soaked in garlic butter. *Estrada do João G Zarco 478 • Map F6 • 291 941 865 • €€€*

4 Coral, Câmara de Lobos
The concrete and glass exterior of this seafront establishment belies a traditional menu that errs towards seafood. *Praça da Autonomia • Map F6 • 291 098 284 • €€*

5 As Vides, Estreito de Câmara de Lobos
You can smell the wood-smoke as you near this 1950s log cabin serving grilled meats from an open fire. *Rua da Achada 17, Sítio da Igreja • Map F6 • 291 945 322 • €€*

6 Sabores do Curral, Curral das Freiras
This charming, rustic eatery offers traditional gastronomical delights of local produce with chestnut as the main ingredient. Try the chestnut liqueur. *Caminho da Igreja 1 • Map F4 • 291 712 257 • Closed Mon • €€*

7 Estalagem Eira do Serrado
Poised 500 m (1640 ft) above Curral das Freiras, you could come here just for the fine view, but the food is also first class, with a good choice of grilled meats and fish. *Eira do Serrado • Map G4 • 291 710 060 • €€€*

8 Casa de Abrigo do Poiso, Poiso Pass
The open fire at this mountain-pass lodge compensates for the cooler high-altitude climate. The glowing embers make delicious barbecued Madeiran kebabs. *Caminho Lombada • Map H4 • 291 782 269 • €€*

9 São Cristóvão, Boaventura
Located along the island's northern central coast, this traditional Portuguese eatery provides a pristine view of the sea and the mountains. *Sitio de São Cristóvão • Map F2 • 291 863 031 • €€*

10 Abrigo do Pastor, Camacha
Hearty mountain fare served in a rustic hunting lodge setting focuses on game, including *javali* (wild boar). *Estrada das Carreiras, Carreiras • Map J5 • 291 922 080 • Closed Tue • €€€*

Left **Paúl da Serra** Right **Seixal**

Western Madeira

THE VALLEY ROAD LINKING RIBEIRA BRAVA AND SÃO VICENTE *via the Encumeada Pass forms the boundary between the high peaks of central Madeira and the flat, treeless moorland of the Paúl da Serra plateau to the west. Scores of ridges and ravines run down the plateau escarpment, like pleats in a skirt. Those to the north plunge almost sheer to the sea, with waterfalls that cascade for hundreds of feet. Farming villages cling to the gentler slopes to the south and west, where new roads are beginning to open up beautiful parts of the island which few visitors have yet explored.*

Porto Moniz

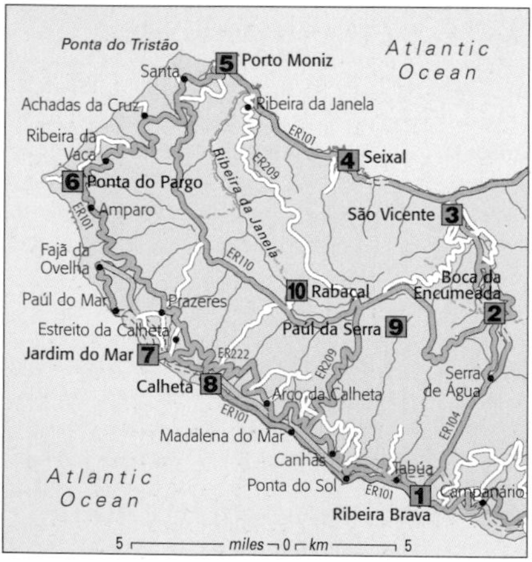

TOP 10 Sights

1. Ribeira Brava
2. Boca da Encumeada
3. São Vicente
4. Seixal
5. Porto Moniz
6. Ponta do Pargo
7. Jardim do Mar
8. Calheta
9. Paúl da Serra
10. Rabaçal

1 Ribeira Brava

Ribeira Brava (literally, "Wild Stream") is one of the island's oldest towns, well established as a centre of sugar production by the 1440s. The large parish church has sculpture from the 1480s. The Museu Etnográfico da Madeira is also worth a visit and has a shop selling Madeiran crafts. *Map D5 • Rodoeste buses 4, 6, 7, 80, 107, 115, 139 and 142 • Museu Etnográfico da Madeira: Rua São Francisco 24; 291 952 598; open 9:30am–5pm Tue–Fri, 10am–12:30pm & 1:30–5:30pm Sat–Sun • Adm charge*

2 Boca da Encumeada

The Encumeada Pass is a saddle of rock dividing the north and south of the island. Clouds from the north often spill over the tip of the mountains, like dry ice pouring from a flask. There are majestic peaks, from Pico Grande in the east to cone-shaped Crista de Galo in the west. Just south of the pass is the Levada do Norte (signposted "Folhadel"), which offers a lovely 15-minute walk to the point where it enters a tunnel. *Map E3 • Rodoeste buses 6 and 139*

3 São Vicente

This pretty village on the northern side of the Encumeada Pass demands to be captured in paint; deep-green shutters, doors and balconies, with stone lintels and frames of ox-blood red, are set in white-walled houses along the grey basalt streets. *Map E2 • Rodoeste buses 6 and 139*

Boca da Encumeada – the view south

São Vicente

4 Seixal

Most of the coastal road now runs through tunnels, but Seixal is one of the few places where you can still get a sense of the north coast's visual splendour. Tall cliffs stretching into the distance are pounded by powerful waves that swell and break at their feet. Vineyards cling to the rock on almost vertical terraces. Waterfalls plunge from the wooded heights on either side of the village. *Map D2 • Rodoeste buses 80 and 139*

5 Porto Moniz

Porto Moniz, the most northwesterly conurbation on the island, combines a bustling agricultural town set high up around its church, with a lower town devoted to food and bathing. Natural rock pools have been turned into a bathing complex offering a safe environment in which to enjoy the exhilarating experience of being showered by spray from waves breaking on the offshore rocks. The landscaped seafront is lined with restaurants selling some of the island's best seafood. *Map B1 • Rodoeste buses 80 and 139*

Lighthouse, Ponta do Pargo

6 Ponta do Pargo

Madeira's westernmost point, Ponta do Pargo is the best place on the island to watch the setting sun or to gaze down at the waves breaking along the tall cliffs of the island's coasts. The lighthouse on the headland dates from the early 20th century and has a small exhibition of maps and photographs charting the history of lighthouses on every island in the Madeiran archipelago. The ceiling of the parish church depicts colourful sunsets, terraced hills, and the scenic spots of the western part of the island, all painted in the 1990s by a Belgian artist who has settled in the village. *Map A2 • Rodoeste buses 80, 139 and 142*

7 Jardim do Mar

This pretty village (literally, "Garden of the Sea") sits at the meeting-point of several ancient cobbled footpaths, which climb up the cliffs to either side. In the village itself, a maze of alleys wind down to a pebble beach, where surfing competitions are held during the winter months. A large sea-wall makes surfing here tricky, even for the very experienced. *Map B4 • Rodoeste bus 142*

Sugar Revival

The sugar mills at Calheta and Porto da Cruz date from the sugar renaissance of the 19th century, when the demand for high-quality sugar rose dramatically, thanks to the popularity of sweetmeats in genteel European households. The nuns of Santa Clara *(see p16)* were especially renowned for their preserves, marzipan sweets, crystallized figs and other delights.

8 Calheta

Calheta's fine parish church, a scaled-down version of Funchal cathedral *(see pp8–9)*, stands on a terrace halfway up the hill leading west out of the village. It has a precious 17th-century ebony-and-silver tabernacle, and a richly decorated *alfarge* (knotwork) ceiling above the high altar. Next door to the church is the Engenho da Calheta, one of Madeira's two surviving sugar mills; the other is in Porto da Cruz *(see p78)*. As well as producing *mel* (honey), used in making the island's unique *bolo de mel* (honey cake), the mill also makes *aguardente* (rum) from distilled cane syrup. *Map B4 • Rodoeste bus 142 • Calheta Church: open 10am–1pm & 4–6pm daily • Engenho da Calheta: 291 822 264; open 8am–7pm Tue–Sun; Free*

9 Paúl da Serra

The undulating plateau of Paúl da Serra ("Mountain Marsh") is the gathering point for the waters that feed many of the island's streams and *levadas*. It serves as a sponge for the abundant rains which fall when clouds reach the island, rise, then cool. Free-range horned cattle graze the lush grass. People from the surrounding villages come here in summer to pick wild bilberries and blackberries, which they turn into delicious conserves. Many of them also depend on the plateau's forest of wind turbines to supply them with electricity. *Map D3 • Rodoeste bus 139*

10 Rabaçal

Washed by centuries of rain running from the flat, monotonous surface of the Paúl da Serra, Rabaçal is a magical green cleft in the moorland. A brisk 2-km (1-mile) walk down a winding tarmac path takes you through stands of heather and broom to a forest house with picnic tables. Rabaçal marks the start of two popular walks (both signposted). One follows the Levada do Risco to the Risco Waterfall (30 minutes there and back); the other follows the next terrace down to 25 Fontes ("25 Springs"), a cauldron-like pool fed by numerous cascades (1 hour 40 minutes there and back). *Map C3 • Rodoeste bus 139*

Risco Falls, Rabaçal

A Day in Western Madeira

Morning

First stop on this long but rewarding trip is **Ribeira Brava**, 25 minutes from Funchal by the south coast highway. If you arrive before the **Ethnography Museum** opens *(see p81)*, enjoy a coffee on the seafront or call in at the church.

Driving north, follow signs to **Serra de Água**. For spectacular mountain views, avoid the new tunnel route to São Vicente.

Descending to **São Vicente**, spare some time for a short but fascinating tour of the lava caves on the east bank of the river.

Take the Erioi Road to **Porto Moniz**. The rock pools of the lower town are a great place to relieve tension after the drive. Follow a dip with lunch in any of the nearby fish restaurants.

Afternoon

Drive back along the road to **São Vicente** for 2 km (1 mile), then turn right to **Ribeira da Janela**. Beyond the village, the road climbs through a wild landscape of native Madeiran forest.

Continue as far as the **Paúl da Serra** plateau. Taking the next two right turns, make for the car park above **Rabaçal**. Allow two hours to explore this woodland world of birdsong, running water, fern-hung rocks and ancient tree heaths.

To return to Funchal, take the **Encumeada Pass**, turn left to **Vargem**, then left again to join the long tunnel that joins the south coast highway at Ribeira Brava.

Left **Ribeira da Janela** Right **Ponta do Sol**

Top 10 Best of the Rest

1 Ribeira da Janela
This wild, uninhabited valley 18 km (11 miles) long, joins the sea beside a rocky islet with a window-like hole (hence the name, "Window Valley"). The road descends through a misty world of ancient trees kept moist by the condensation of clouds. *Map C1*

2 Fanal
This forest house halfway up the Ribeira de Janela is the starting point for walks that lead through an alpine landscape of herb-rich meadows, filled with ancient laurel trees. *Map C2*

3 Ponta do Sol
American novelist John dos Passos (1896–1970) visited this village in 1960 to see his grandparents' house – now a cultural centre. *Rua Príncipe Dom Luís 3 • Map D5 • 291 974 034*

4 Lombada
On a ridge above Ponta do Sol is one of Madeira's oldest houses – the 15th-century mansion of Columbus's friend João Esmeraldo *(see p65)*. The watermill opposite is fed by one of the island's oldest *levadas*. A pretty church of 1722 is lined with tile pictures of the Virtues. *Map D5*

5 Arco da Calheta
Another early church survives at the heart of this sprawling village – the mid-15th-century Capela do Loreto, founded by the wife of Zarco's grandson. *Map C4*

6 Lombo dos Reis
The "Ridge of the Kings" is named after the tiny, rustic Capela dos Reis Magos ("Chapel of the Three Kings"), which has a rare early 16th-century Flemish altar carving of the Nativity. *Map B4*

7 Lugar de Baixo
Above the tiny freshwater lagoon at Lugar de Baixo is a visitor centre with pictures of the wild birds that frequent this rocky shore, though you are more likely to see domesticated ducks and moorhens. *Map D5*

8 Prazeres
The priest at Prazeres has established a small children's farm opposite the church, but the main attraction is the flower-lined path along the Levada Nova ("New Levada"), which can be followed east or west. *Map B3*

9 Paúl do Mar
The best approach to this fishing (and surfing) village is down the twisting road from Fajã de Orvela. On the way, look out for a glimpse of the stunning Galinas Gorge. *Map A3*

10 Cristo Rei
This statue of Christ (on the ER209 road to Paúl da Serra) is reminiscent of the famous one in Rio de Janeiro. It is also the starting point for easy *levada* walks – west to the Paúl da Serra, east to the waterfalls at Cascalho. *Map D4*

O Cachalote, Porto Moniz

Price Categories

For a three course meal for one with half a bottle of wine (or equivalent meal), taxes and extra charges.

€	under €15
€€	€15–€25
€€€	€25–€40
€€€€	€40–€60
€€€€€	over €60

TOP 10 Places to Eat

1 Pousada dos Vinháticos, Serra de Água

The food is perfectly good but the views steal the limelight. Picture windows look out onto Madeira's most Wagnerian mountain landscapes, lit by the setting sun. *Map E4 • 291 952 344 • €€€*

2 O Virgílio, São Vicente

"Virgil's" stands out from the other seafront fish restaurants in São Vicente for its eccentric decor, authentic Madeiran atmosphere and perfect sardines. *Map E2 • 291 842 467 • €€*

3 O Cachalote, Porto Moniz

Long regarded as the best seafood restaurant in Porto Moniz, O Cachalote now has competition from several other restaurants in this popular resort. *Praia do Porto Moniz • Map B1 • 291 853 180 • Closed D daily • €€€€*

4 Orca, Porto Moniz

The circular dining room with its big windows maximizes the views over the rock pools of Porto Moniz, adding savour to a menu that features *caldeirada* (fish casserole), red bream and sea bass. *Praia do Porto Moniz • Map B1 • 291 850 000 • €€€*

5 Casa de Chá "O Fío", Ponta do Pargo

A teahouse isn't what you'd expect to find on a clifftop, but many make the pilgrimage for homemade soups and light meals. *Sitio do Salão de Baixo • Map A2 • 291 882 525 • €€*

6 Jardim Atlântico, Prazeres

The best bet for vegetarians looking for an escape from an endless diet of omelettes, the restaurant at the Jardim Atlântico Hotel sources its produce from local market gardens. *Lombo da Rocha • Map B3 • 291 820 220 • €€*

7 O Manjerico, Arco da Calheta

Renowned for its stuffed chicken, this homely eatery is a little off the beaten track but well worth the diversion. Call ahead for reservations. *Caminho da Referta, Pico Prazeres • Map B3 • 291 822 897 • €*

8 Solar dos Prazeres, Prazeres

Enjoy splendid ocean and mountain views while savouring grilled cod and *espetada de carne* (grilled meat kebab) at this popular eatery. *Lombo da Rocha • Map B3 • 291 822 759 • €€*

9 Cantinho da Madalena

Grab a seat on the terrace and enjoy a typical Madeiran meal at this local favourite. *Avenida 1 de Fevereio 2, Madalena do Mar • Map C4 • 291 972 235 • €€€*

10 Borda D'Água, Ribeira Brava

Wholesome fresh fish and seafood characterizes the menu at this popular oceanfront venue. Vegetarian options are also available. *Rua Engenheiro Ribeiro Pereira • Map D5 • 291 957 697 • Dis access • €€*

Left **Santa Cruz** Right **Machico's fortress**

Eastern Madeira

MOST VISITORS CATCH A GLIMPSE OF EASTERN MADEIRA *as they arrive, flying in over Machico, the island's second biggest town, and driving from the airport to Funchal along the south coast highway. Away from these areas, there are wide expanses of untamed nature where no roads go. These include the whole north coast, with its exhilarating paths and vertigo-inducing cliffs. Also worth seeking out are the historic whaling village of Caniçal, the charming town of Santa Cruz and the gentle, pastoral landscape of the Santo da Serra plateau, source of the island's wicker products.*

Coastal view of the Garajau

Top 10 Sights

1. Garajau
2. Caniço de Baixo
3. Santa Cruz
4. Machico
5. Caniçal
6. Ponta de São Lourenço
7. The Ilhas Desertas
8. Portela
9. Santo António da Serra
10. Camacha

1 Garajau

A miniature version of Rio de Janeiro's statue of Christ the Redeemer was erected on the wild and rocky headland at the southern end of the village in 1927. The terns (*garajau* in Portuguese) that gave their name to the village can still be seen from the zigzag path that winds down the cliff face to a pebble beach below the headland. Underwater caves and reefs rich in marine life extend for 2 km (1 mile) to either side, and are protected as a marine reserve *(see p90)*. ✎ *Map J6*

Statue of Christ the Redeemer, Garajau

2 Caniço de Baixo

Before heading to this charming clifftop holiday village, stop to admire fine Baroque decoration at Caniço's 18th-century Igreja Matriz in Rua Jão Paulo II. The tiny Praia da Canavieira public beach is reached down an easily-missed alley near the junction with Rua da Falésia. For a small sum, you can also use the Galomar Lido (open 9am–7pm summer, 10am–5pm winter). The lido is the base for the Manta Diving Centre, which organizes trips to the Garajau Marine Reserve *(see above)*. ✎ *Map J6*

Galomar Lido, Caniço de Baixo

3 Santa Cruz

Santa Cruz is a town of great character, and surprisingly peaceful, given that the airport runway is right next door. The focal point is the beach, lined with cafés and *pastelarias* (pastry shops), as well as the Art Deco-style Palm Beach Lido, painted azure and cream. Back from the coast and down winding alleys is a 15th-century Gothic church as splendid as the cathedral in Funchal, and perhaps designed by the same architect *(see p8)*. ✎ *Map K5 • SAM bus 20, 23, 53, 60, 78, 113,156*

4 Machico

Machico is where Captain Zarco and his crew first set foot on Madeira in 1420. The chapel they founded *(see p40)* is on the eastern side of the harbour, shaded by giant Indian fig trees. A statue of Machico's first governor, Tristão Vaz Teixeira, stands in front of the fine 15th-century parish church on the main square. A grid of cobbled alleys leads from here down to the seafront fortress. ✎ *Map K4 • SAM bus 20, 23, 53, 78, 113,156*

5 Caniçal

Caniçal holds the dubious honour of being a former whaling port. In 1956, John Huston came here to shoot the opening scenes of *Moby Dick*, but its star, Gregory Peck, became so seasick that they had to shoot the rest in a studio. The Museu da Baleia *(see p38)* explains how conservation has replaced whaling.

✎ *Map L4 • SAM bus 113*

• Museu da Baleia: Rua da Praia D'Eira. 291 961 858. Adm charge

Volcanic cliffs at Ponta de São Lourenço

6 Ponta de São Lourenço

The long, narrow chain of eroded volcanic cliffs and ravines at the eastern tip of Madeira is an exciting and dramatic wilderness, protected as a nature reserve because of its coastal plants. The rocky peninsula can be explored from the much-used path that starts from the car park located at the end of the south coast road.
Map M4

7 The Ilhas Desertas

Ponta de São Lourenço is linked underwater to the offshore Ilhas Desertas ("Desert Isles"), which form part of the same volcanic formation. Though arid and uninhabited, these islands nevertheless host all sorts of rare and endangered wildlife, including spiders, monk seals, petrels and shearwaters. An application has been made to UNESCO to have the islands declared a World Natural Heritage Site. For a closer look, contact one of the boat companies based at Funchal's marina, many of which offer day-long trips to the islands *(see p48)*. *Map J1*

The Ilhas Selvagens

Also part of the Madeiran archipelago are the arid and treeless Ilhas Selvagens ("Wild Islands"), which lie 285 km (178 miles) south of Madeira and 165 km (103 miles) north of Tenerife, in the Canaries. These tiny volcanic islets, claimed by Portugal in 1458, have Europe's largest nesting colonies of rare shearwaters and storm-petrels. Since 1976, military sentries from the Nature Guards team have been permanently stationed on the islands to protect the birds, which were once caught, salted and dried as a delicacy.

8 Portela

The viewing point at Portela has more than its fair share of roadside cafés because it was once the transport hub for the east of the island. Tunnels linking São Roque do Faial with Machico have changed all that, but Portela is still an important landmark for walkers. You can walk south from here to Porto da Cruz *(see p78)* along a trail once used by wine carriers, or west along the Levada do Portela through dense primeval woodland and mountain scenery to Ribeiro Frio *(see p76)*. *Map J4*
• SAM bus 53, 78

9 Santo António da Serra

The village of Santo António da Serra (known to Madeirans simply as Santo da Serra), sits in the middle of a plateau flat enough for golf courses *(see p48)* and fields of grazing cows. Despite its frequent cloud cover, wealthy English merchants once built rural homes here: one of the former homes of the Blandy family *(see p25)* is now a public park with camellias, hydrangeas, rhododendrons, deer and horse enclosures, and viewing points that look out toward Ponta de São Lourenço. *Map J4 • Carros de São Gonçalo bus 77*

10 Camacha

A monument in the centre of Camacha proudly declares that Portugal's first ever game of football was played in the town in 1875, organized by an English schoolboy. However, it is the O Relógio ("The Clock") wicker factory opposite *(see p56)* that draws people here, rather than its soccer history. You can see demonstrations of wicker-making in the workshop. If you explore the back streets of the village, you can spot the raw material: stacks of freshly cut willow canes. These are steeped in water and stripped of their bark, before being boiled to make them pliable enough to weave. *Map J5 • Carros de São Gonçalo bus 77, 110, 129*

O Relógio wicker workshop, Camacha

A Day in Eastern Madeira

Morning

Assuming you are staying in Funchal, start off by getting onto the south coast highway (follow signs to the airport), then take the São Gonçalo exit and head for Camacha. The road passes the Quinta do Palheiro Ferreiro gardens *(see p24)*. **Camacha** is famous for its wicker. Head to the workshop on the main square for an insight into how they are constructed *(see p56)*.

Carry on to **Santo António da Serra** for a walk in the wooded park. Then continue through the village and turn left where the road forks for **Machico** *(see p87)*, with its churches and fortress. Depending on the time, you might want to stop in **Caniçal** *(see p87)* for lunch and to see the Museu da Baleia *(see p38)*, devoted to the subject of whales.

Afternoon

About 3 km (2 miles) east of Caniçal, you will reach a car park marked "Prainha". Follow the path down to Madeira's only natural sand beach, perfect for a swim.

At the mini-roundabout just beyond the car park, turn left and you will come to a head-spinning viewpoint. Back at the roundabout, turn left again and continue to a large car park. From here, you can sample the first part of the path that leads across the treeless peninsula to the east of the island. Head back toward Funchal and leave the south coast highway at **Santa Cruz** *(see p87)*, where you will find a good choice of restaurants for dinner.

Bottle-nosed dolphins

Top 10 Garajau Marine Reserve Sights

1 Monk Seal
Europe's most endangered mammal, the monk seal was once persecuted by Madeiran fishermen. The small surviving colony is now protected, but can be seen on trips to the Ilhas Desertas *(see p88)*.

2 Sperm Whale
Canićal's fishermen caught their last sperm whale in 1981. This is the whale you are most likely to see on whale-watching trips *(see p52)*.

3 Humpback Whale
The humpback loves to leap out of the water and perform acrobatic somersaults (known as "breaching"). Madeirans can regularly spot this graceful whale offshore during the winter. A mere 20,000 remain in existence.

4 Pilot Whales
Large schools of pilot whales use Madeira as a migration route as they pass between the subtropical waters of the Canary Islands on their way north to the Arctic, though their precise route remains a mystery.

5 Killer Whales
Despite their name, these big whales (the largest members of the dolphin family) have never been known to attack humans – they are more likely to attack other whales. Solitary killer whales can often be spotted patrolling Madeira's warm waters.

6 Common Dolphin
No longer as common as their name suggests. Population numbers of these endangered mammals have bounced back, however, since the creation of Madeira's ocean marine reserve.

7 Bottle-nosed Dolphin
The bottle-nosed dolphin is another sea mammal that has benefited from the creation of the reserve, which stretches 200,000 km sq (77,200 sq miles) from eastern Madeira to the Ilhas Selvagens ("Wild Islands"), a group of uninhabited rocks north of the Canary Islands.

8 Gulls
Herring gulls and western yellow-legged gulls are the seabirds you are most likely to see on boat trips or hanging around fishing ports such as Canićal or Funchal.

9 Common Terns
Related to gulls, but with a deeply forked tail and a graceful flight, Common terns can be seen from the lookout point at Garajau, skimming the water and diving for small fish.

10 Shearwaters
The shearwater is able to glide just above the waves, scarcely moving its wings. Once it was hunted by fishermen, who regarded it as a delicacy. Madeira has more than six varieties, including the Great Shearwater.

To know more about exploring Garajau Marine Reserve, visit www.portugaldiving.com

Mercado Velha, Machico

Price Categories

For a three course meal for one with half a bottle of wine (or equivalent meal), taxes and extra charges.	
€	under €15
€€	€15–€25
€€€	€25–€40
€€€€	€40–€60
€€€€€	over €60

Top 10 Places to Eat

1 Figos, Garajau
This stylish bistro bar offers an authentic regional menu alongside contemporary Mediterranean options, such as *pasta al pomodoro.* *Rua da Olaria 69 • Map J6 • 291 934 004 • Dis access • Open D daily • €€€*

2 Sapori di Napoli, Santa Cruz
This popular Italian restaurant and pizzeria serves delicious pastas and a range of traditional fish and meat dishes. A takeaway option is also available. *Avenida 25 de Junho • Map K5 • 291 522 227 • €€*

3 La Perla, Caniço de Baixo
Dishes such as seafood *risotto au champagne* and fillet of veal with rosemary exemplify the international à la carte menu. *Quinta Splendida Hotel, Estrada da Ponta Oliveira 11 • Map J6 • 291 930 400 • Open D Wed–Sun • €€€€*

4 Gallery, Caniço de Baixo
The Inn and Art hotel's restaurant is a hit with vegetarians, for whom there's a special dish of the day and a range of salads. The fish is grilled on a eucalyptus wood fire. *Rua Robert Baden Powell 61/2 • Map J6 • 291 938 200 • €€€€*

5 Avó Micas, Santo da Serra
Traditional Madeiran dishes, such as pork marinated in wine and garlic, are served at this teahouse-style restaurant. *Porto Bay Serra Golf Hotel, Sítio dos Casais Próximos • Map J4 • 291 550 500 • €€€€*

6 Bar Amarelo, Caniçal
Among the buildings of Caniçal, the cream-coloured limestone-and-steel decor of this harbourside gem stands out. Choose from salads, pasta or grilled fish. *Caniçal • Map L4 • 291 961 798 • €€*

7 Mercado Velho, Machico
The courtyard of the old seafront market in Machico has been turned into an al fresco restaurant serving grilled fish and meat. *Rua do Mercado • Map K4 • 291 965 926 • €€*

8 O Relógio, Camacha
Come here on Saturday to see one of Madeira's top folk song-and-dance acts. As well as local dishes, there are specials, such as smoked fish, and grilled prawns in a chilli and garlic sauce. *Largo Conselheiro Aires de Ornelas 12 • Map J5 • 291 922 777 • €€*

9 Praia dos Reis Magos
This simplest of beachside restaurants within feet of the shore serves the local fishermen's daily catch. *Praia dos Reis Magos (1 km (half a mile) east of Caniço de Baixo) • Map J6 • 291 934 345 • €€*

10 Miradouro de Portela, Portela
This homely restaurant with warming fires serves generous portions of herb-flavoured beef kebabs and tomato soup. *Portela • Map J4 • 291 966 169 • Closed Mon • €€*

Left **Porto Santo's beach** Right **Church of Nossa Senhora da Piedade, Vila Baleira**

Porto Santo

PORTO SANTO LIES *43 km (27 miles) northeast of Madeira. Zarco (see p15) and his crew took shelter here in 1418, while on their way to explore the west coast of Africa. Realizing that the island would be a useful base, he returned here in 1419 to plant the Portuguese flag, going on to Madeira the following year. Early settlers introduced rabbits and goats, which quickly stripped the island of its vegetation, so Porto Santo is not as green as Madeira. Instead, the "Golden Island" has one major asset: its magnificent sandy beach, which brings holiday-makers from Madeira and mainland Europe in search of sunshine, sea and the agreeable sense of being a very long way from the busy world.*

View from Ponta da Calheta, the island's westernmost point

TOP 10 Sights

1. The Beach
2. Vila Baleira
3. Nossa Senhora da Piedade
4. Casa Museu Cristóvão Colombo
5. The Jetty
6. Pico de Ana Ferreira
7. Ponta da Calheta
8. Zimbralinho
9. Fonte da Areia
10. Pico do Castelo

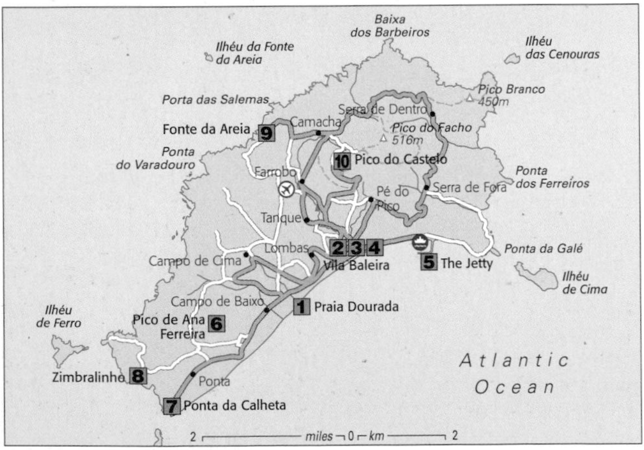

Preceding pages **Typical tile picture on the building of the Ritz Restaurant, Funchal**

The old town of Vila Baleira, capital of Porto Santo

1 The Beach

On top of Porto Santo's volcanic rocks, limestone, sandstone and coral were laid down millions of years ago, beneath a warm, shallow sea. Falling sea levels exposed the coral to erosion, and the result is the magnificent 10-km (6-mile) sweep of sand that runs along the southern side of the island. Backed by dunes and tamarisk trees, the sand is divided into several beach areas, of which Fontinha and Ribeiro Salgado have been awarded Blue Flag status for environmental quality. Enjoying the beach may have therapeutic benefits: burying yourself in the sand is said to bring relief from rheumatism and arthritis. *Map L2*

2 Vila Baleira

All life on the island centres on the capital, which sits roughly halfway along the southern coast. Pavement cafés fill the main square, Largo do Pelourinho ("Pillory Square"), where offenders were once punished and public proclamations read out. The town hall, with its double staircase flanked by dragon trees, stands on the site of the pillory. The cobbled pavement in front has a glass-topped, stone-lined pit, which was once used for storing grain. *Map L2*

3 Nossa Senhora da Piedade

To the east of the main square in Vila Baleira stands the majestic parish church, Nossa Senhora da Piedade, completed in 1446. Gothic rib-vaulting and rainwater spouts carved with human and animal heads have survived from this earlier church, which was torched by pirates, then rebuilt in 1667. The 17th-century altar painting of Christ being laid in his tomb is by Martím Conrado. The saints on either side were painted in 1945 by German artist Max Romer *(see p13)*. *Map L2*

4 Casa Museu Cristóvão Colombo

Christopher Columbus (1451–1506) came to Madeira in 1478 as the agent for a Lisbon sugar merchant. He married Filipa Moniz, daughter of the governor of Porto Santo, but she died soon after their son was born in 1479 and Columbus left the islands in 1480. The house where they are said to have lived is now a museum, displaying portraits of Columbus, maps of his voyages and models of his vessels.

Travessa da Sacristia 2–4 • Map L2 • 291 983 405 • Open 10am–12:30pm & 2–5:30pm Tue–Sat (until 7pm Jul, Aug & Sep), 10am–1pm Sun • Adm charge • www.museucolombo-portosanto.com

Casa Museu Cristóvão Colombo

For details of flights and ferries to Port Santo **See p103**

Water, Wine and Lime

Water, wine and lime were once Porto Santo's economic staples. Mineral water was bottled at the disused factory opposite the Torre Praia Hotel access road. Quicklime (used in mortar) made in lime kilns like the one at the Torre Praia was exported to Madeira and beyond. You can still buy Listrão Branco, the local fortified wine, but less is made every year.

5 The Jetty

The palm-lined path leading from the centre of Vila Baleira to the seafront is flanked by landscaped gardens dotted with rusty cannons. There are also memorials to Columbus (a bust set on a pedestal), to the 16th-century soldiers and sailors who colonized Madeira (an obelisk carved with abstract figures), and to the sailors who used to risk their lives crossing heavy seas to keep Porto Santo supplied with food and firewood (a bronze statue of a sailor at the rudder of a boat). *Map L2*

6 Pico de Ana Ferreira

Porto Santo consists of a saddle of land between two groups of cone-shaped volcanic peaks. At 283 m (929 ft), the Pico de Ana Ferreira is the highest of the summits at the more developed western end of the island. A road up its southern slopes will take you as far as the 17th-century Church of São Pedro. From there, a track leads around the peak to a disused quarry featuring an interesting formation of prismatic basalt columns aptly known as the "Organ Pipes". *Map L2*

Basalt structures on Pico de Ana Ferreira

7 Ponta da Calheta

The westernmost tip of the island is a beautiful spot, with a series of secluded sandy coves reached by scrambling over wave-eroded rocks. From the bar and restaurant at the end of the coast road, you can look across to Ilhéu de Baixo, the large, uninhabited rocky islet southwest of Porto Santo. Madeira, too, is visible on the distant horizon, resembling a huge whale, and usually capped by clouds. *Map K2*

The rugged coastline and azure waters of Zimbralinho

8 Zimbralinho

Zimbralinho is the most beautiful of all the little rocky coves nestling along the western flank of the island, its transparent blue seas popular with swimmers and divers. The cove is at its best around lunchtime, as it is shaded earlier and later in the day.

If you enjoy walking, buy the Guide to the Paths and Routes of the Island of Porto Santo *from local shops or the tourist office.*

Wind-eroded cliffs, Fonte da Areia

The path to the cove starts at the end of the road that leads to the Centro Hipico *(see p98)*, at the western end of the island. *Map K2*

9 Fonte da Areia

Water once bubbled straight out of the sandstone cliffs at Fonte da Areia ("Fountain of Sand"), but in 1843, the spring was tamed, and you can now taste the natural, rock-filtered mineral water by simply turning a tap. The path to the spring leads down a wind-eroded gully, where the cliffs have been sculpted into laminated sheets of harder and softer rock. Lovers have carved their names on the rock face, but so ferocious is the scouring wind that declarations of perpetual love inscribed ten years ago are now growing faint. *Map L1*

10 Pico do Castelo

The high peak to the east of Vila Baleira is called Castle Peak, though despite its name, it was never fortified. From the 15th century on, it was used as a place of refuge whenever pirates threatened to attack. It was equipped with a cannon, which still survives at the lookout point near the summit. A cobbled road takes you all the way to the lookout, past the cypress, cedar and pine trees that have been planted to turn the slopes from sandy to green. *Map L1*

A Day on Porto Santo

Morning

You should ideally hire a car *(see p98)* for this tour, though you could do it by taxi. Start by driving northeast out of **Vila Baleira** *(see p95)*, up to the viewing point at Portela. Nearby, you will see three windmills of a type once common on Porto Santo. Carry on around the eastern end of the island, until a turning to the right takes you down to Serra de Fora beach. Some 2 km (1 mile) further north are traditional stone houses at Serra de Dentro and fine views from Pico Branco.

At the Camacha crossroads, a drivable track to the left leads up **Pico do Castelo**, soon turning into a stone-paved road. The viewing point at the top has great views over central Porto Santo. Back down at Camacha, there is a choice of cafés and bars for lunch.

Afternoon

First stop after lunch is **Fonte da Areia**. Despite looking arid, Porto Santo has several natural springs like this one. Next, head on toward Campo de Cima. As you drive alongside the airport runway, you will see some of the few vineyards left on the island that still produce wine.

Take the road up **Pico de Ana Ferreira**, then continue on foot to see its extraordinary-looking basalt columns. Afterwards, drive on to the stunning westernmost tip of the island, **Ponta da Calheta**. You should have plenty of time for relaxing on the sand, a swim, or a drink at the beach bar, before returning to Vila Baleira.

Left **Shopping at the Centro Artesanato** Right **Beachcombing**

TOP 10 Activities

1 Sightseeing
Take a tour in an open-top bus to get a feel for the island. Two-hour tours depart daily at 2pm from the bus stop by the petrol station on the eastern side of the jetty. *Map L2*

2 Exploring by Car
Taxis offer island tours, but if you prefer to explore independently, you can hire a car for the day from Moinho Rent-a-Car. *Map L2 • 291 982 141*

3 Exploring by Bike
Auto Acessórios Colombo (opposite the road to the Torre Praia Hotel) rents out bicycles, scooters and quad bikes. Bikes can also be hired in advance from Porto Santo Line *(see p103)*. Upon arrival at Porto Santo, pick up a bike at the quay, returning it before the voyage back to Madeira. *Auto Acessórios Colombo: Map L2; 291 984 438 • Porto Santo Line: 291 210 300*

4 Beachcombing
Take a leisurely stroll along the unbroken sands from Vila Baleira to Ponta da Calheta *(see p96)*. Tropical shells often wash up on the shore. *Map L2*

5 Watersports
Mar Dourado, located at Praia da Fontinha beach below the Torre Praia Hotel, rents out pedalos and kayaks, and will organize paragliding, water skiing, windsurfing and boat trips. *Mar Dourado • 963 970 789 • Map L2*

6 Tennis
Porto Santo Tennis Academy, located next to the golf course, is fully equipped to competition standard. The main stadium has six courts that are accessible to the public when not being used for tournaments. *Porto Santo Tennis Academy • Campo de Baixo • Map L2 • 291 983 274*

7 Diving
Thanks to unpolluted seas and the absence of commercial fishing, Porto Santo's shores are rich in marine life. Try Porto Santo Sub, based at the marina, or Rhea Dive at Rua Dr José Diamantino Lima. *Porto Santo Sub: Map L2; 916 033 997 • Rhea Dive: Map L2; 964 500 557*

8 Horse riding
Porto Santo's Hipicenter (Equestrian Centre) takes children and adults at all levels. *Sítio da Ponta • Map K2 • 291 983 258*

9 Golf
Designed by Severiano Ballesteros, Porto Santo Golfe has an 18-hole, par 72 course and a 9-hole, par 3 pitch-and-putt course. *Sitio das Marinhas • Map L2 • 291 983 778*

10 Shopping
Shells, model ships and other souvenirs with a nautical theme are the stock-in-trade of Port Santo's craft shops, which you will find located in the Centro do Artesanato, next to the jetty. *Map L2*

Left **Pestana Porto Santo** Right **Ponta da Calheta**

TOP 10 Places to Eat and Stay

1 Pé na Água, Vila Baleira

Not quite "foot in water" as the name suggests, but you are right by the sand at this board-walk spot. The chef cooks a great seafood rice, as well as grilled fish and beef kebabs. *Sitio das Pedras Pretas (beyond the Torre Praia Hotel) • Map L2 • 291 985 242 • €€€€*

2 Vila Alencastre, Porto Santo

Filete de peixe-espada com banana (swordfish fillet with banana) and *arroz de pato* (duck rice) are specialities at this rustic eatery. *Estrada do Forno do Cal, Campo de Baixo • Map L2 • 291 985 072 • €€€*

3 Ponta da Calheta, Calheta

The "Sunset Bar" has an enviable position at the western end of the island, where you can sip cocktails and enjoy garlic-rich prawns and clams. *Map K2 • 291 985 322 • €€€*

4 Quinta do Serrado, Porto Santo

This hotel-restaurant serves hearty fare, such as pork loin with bacon and coriander sauce. The passion fruit pudding is a delight. Excellent wine list. *Hotel Quinta do Serrado, Sítio do Pedregal • Map L1 • 291 980 270 • €€€*

5 Baiana, Vila Baleira

Join the locals at this popular restaurant. Of the many fish caught daily, there's bound to be one you haven't tried. *Rua Dr Nuno S Teixeira 9 • Map L2 • 291 984 649 • €€€*

6 Salinas, Vila Baleira

Signature dishes at this stylish oceanfront eatery include mixed grill kebab with banana and octopus stew. *Rua Goulart Medeiros (part of the Torre Praia Hotel) • Map L2 • 291 980 450 • €€€*

7 Pestana Porto Santo, Porto Santo

At this upmarket all inclusive family resort and spa complex, 275 rooms, suites and private apartments, encircle landscaped gardens and two pool areas. The four on-site restaurants include a buffet and à la carte Mediterranean. *Estrada Regional 111/120, Sítio do Campo de Baixo • Map L2 • 291 144 000 • www.pestana.com • €€€€€*

8 Torre Praia, Vila Baleira

With a cocktail bar in the tower, and an atrium built around a historic lime kiln, the Hotel Torre Praia has plenty of character. *Rua Goulart Medeiros • Map L2 • 291 980 450 • www.portosantohotels.com • €€€*

9 Luamar ApartHotel, Cabeço da Ponta

Located 4 km (2 miles) west of Vila Baleira, the Luamar is the island's best self-catering choice. *Map L2 • 291 980 190 • www.portosantohotels.com • €€€*

10 Pensão Central, Vila Baleira

The Central is a bright and friendly hotel whose only drawback is the short climb from the town centre. *Rua Coronel A M Vasconcelos • Map L2 • 291 982 226 • €€*

For a guide to restaurant and hotel price ranges **See p71 and p113 respectively**

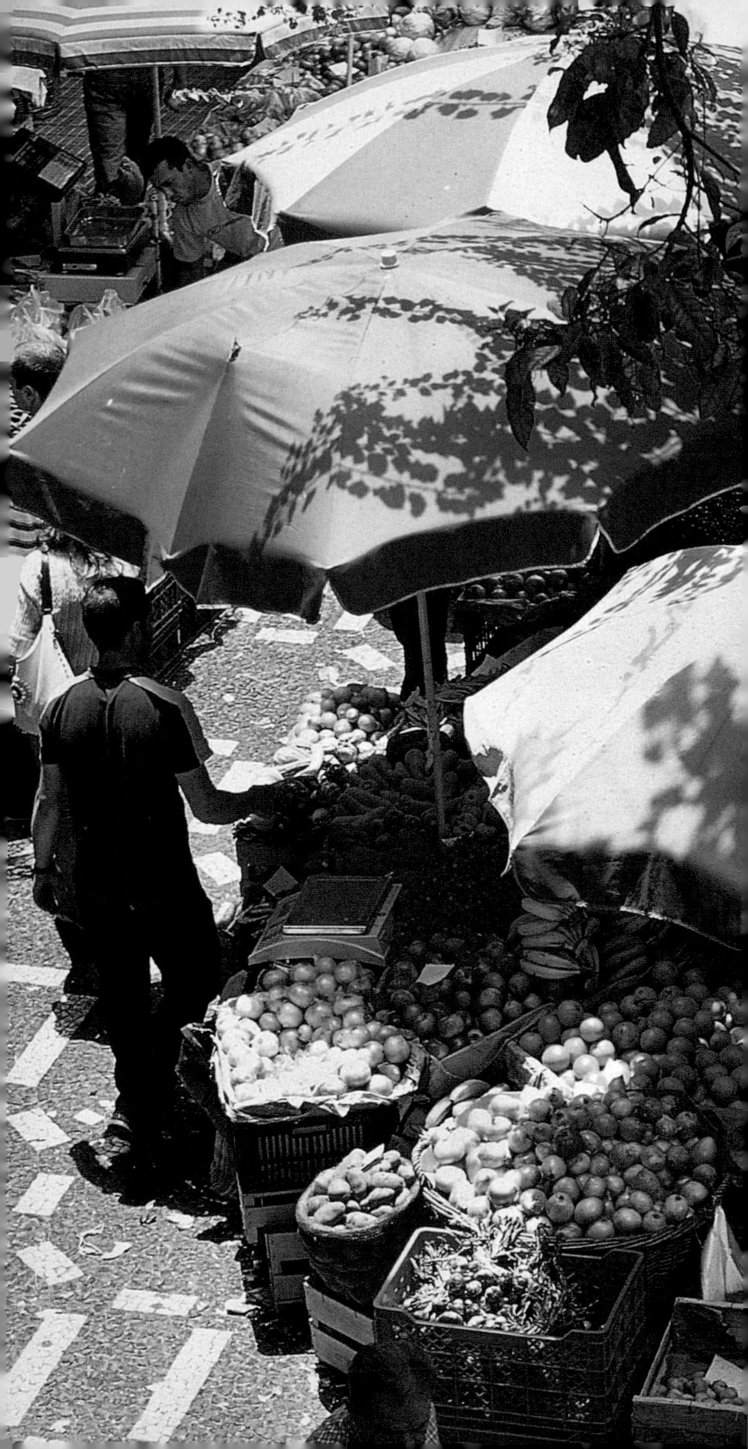

STREETSMART

Left **Casually dressed tourists enjoy al fresco dining** Right **Christmas, peak season on Madeira**

10 General Information

1 When to Go

Christmas is peak season; hotels charge double their normal rates. Easter, July and August are also busy. June is surprisingly quiet, and enjoys perfect weather. Madeira has a generally mild subtropical climate, with average temperatures ranging from 17° C (62° F) in February to 23° C (75° F) in September. October to March sees the highest rainfall, especially on the northern side of the island. Porto Santo tends to be fine throughout the year.

2 What to Pack

Even in winter, it is warm enough to eat out of doors during the day, so you will need light clothes, with extra layers for nights and the cooler mountains. Casual wear is the norm. If you intend to walk, bring a torch (flashlight), waterproofs and non-slip shoes.

3 Tourist Offices

The Portuguese tourist office has branches in most countries and offers useful information on Madeira. The Madeira tourist board's website is excellent and frequently updated. Funchal's main tourist office provides Funchal street maps and details of bus services.
Madeira Board of Tourism: Avenida Arriaga 16, Funchal. Map P3. 291 211 902. Open 9am–8pm Mon–Fri, 9am–4:30pm Sat & Sun. www.visitmadeira.pt

4 Passports and Visas

Visitors can stay on Madeira for 90 days with a valid passport or recognized EU identity card and an onward or return ticket. There are no embassies on the island itself (they are all located in Lisbon). Several consulates are located in Funchal *(see box)*.

5 Customs

As part of the European Union, Madeira imposes virtually no restrictions on imports of cigarettes and alcohol from other EU member states, as long as they are for private consumption.

6 Public Holidays

Everything closes on 25 Dec, 1 Jan and throughout Easter. The following are also holidays: Shrove Tuesday, 25 April, 1 May, 10 June, 15 Aug and 8 Dec. Shops and offices close on public holidays; large supermarkets stay open, as do businesses aimed at tourists.

7 Electricity and Water

The electricity supply is 220 volts AC. Sockets accept plugs with two round pins. Transformers are required for 110-volt devices, and adaptors for non-continental plugs. Tap water is safe to drink; mineral water is cheap and readily available.

8 Opening Hours

Shops trade from 9am–7pm on weekdays and from 9am–1pm on Saturdays. Large supermarkets stay open until 10pm every day. Banks are open weekdays from 8:30am–3pm. Most museums are shut from noon on Saturday until Tuesday; a few are open on Sunday mornings. Churches mainly open from 8am–noon and again from 4–7pm.

9 Time Differences

Madeira observes exactly the same time as the UK, throughout the year. At noon on Madeira, it is 7am in New York and 4am in Los Angeles.

10 Language

Most Madeirans can converse in English. Many can also manage common French and German phrases, in addition to their native Portuguese.

Consulates in Funchal

Belgium *291 210 200*
France *291 200 750*
Germany *291 220 338*
Italy *291 223 890*
Netherlands *291 703 803*
Norway *291 741 515*
South Africa *291 223 521*
Sweden *291 707 700*
UK *291 212 860*
USA *217 273 300*

Preceding pages **Stalls at Funchal's Mercado dos Lavradores**

Left **Cruise ship** Right **Plane at Porto Santo's airport**

TOP 10 Getting to and Around Madeira

1 By Air From Europe

TAP Air Portugal operates scheduled flights (direct or via Lisbon) from major European hubs. Online travel agents, such as Expedia, are the quickest way to check flights and prices. Charter flights are operated by carriers such as easyJet, Thomsonfly and Jet2 and are usually cheaper. However, some offers may only be available as part of a package or during the summer. *TAP Air Portugal: www.flytap.com • easyJet: www.easyjet.com • Thomsonfly: www.thomsonfly.com • Jet2: www.jet2.com*

2 By Air From the Americas

As there are no direct flights from the US, you will fly into Lisbon, then continue on the 90-minute onward leg to Madeira.

3 Madeira Airport

Madeira's airport has a modern terminal building with shops, cafés, car rental offices and banking facilities. An airport bus departs for Funchal at roughly 90-minute intervals, but its schedules do not always coincide with flights. *Map K5 • 291 520 700 • www.anam.pt*

4 By Sea

Car ferries no longer operate between Madeira and mainland Portugal. Madeira features on a number of cruise itineraries, but passengers usually spend only a few hours in port.

5 Taxis

Madeira's yellow taxis are ubiquitous and convenient. Drivers have to display a table of fixed charges (for trips such as that from the airport to Funchal), and must use their meters on other journeys. You can also use taxis for half- and whole-day tours of the island: make sure you agree a rate in advance, or refer to the price list on www.aitram.pt.

6 Buses

Buses are an easy, economical way of getting around the island, though services are geared to the peak commuter hours of 8–10am and 4–7pm. The environmental- and wheelchair-friendly Linha Eco minibuses operate in Funchal. For timetable information, visit www.horariosdofunchal.pt.

7 Car Rental

For flexibility, hire a car. If you do this, however, be aware that parking in Funchal is difficult and metered. Underground car parks are the most convenient option. Local companies, such as Auto Jardim and Rodavante, can offer cheaper deals than international franchises. *Auto Jardim: 291 524 023; www.auto-jardim.com • Rodavante: 291 524 718; www.rodavante.com*

8 Rules of the Road

Madeira's roads are improving, but be careful when you join a fast highway from a slip road. You may have difficulty getting above second gear on one of the island's older roads, which tend to be steep and winding. Parked cars, buses and pedestrians are everywhere, so drive with caution. If another driver flashes his lights, he is proceeding, not giving way.

9 Porto Santo by Air

Flights to Porto Santo from Madeira Airport depart at one- or two-hour intervals. The trip takes 15 minutes; you can check in up to 45 minutes before departure. Tickets can be booked online or through any travel agent. They cost from €117–€158 return. *Aerovip Contact Centre: 291 106 976; www.aerovip.pt*

10 Porto Santo by Sea

The sea journey, by modern car ferry equipped with cinema, restaurants, shops and first- and second-class lounges, takes two-and-a-half hours. Ships leave Funchal at 8am, returning at 9.30pm. Tickets can be booked through travel agents and official kiosks, or bought at the port before boarding. The cost is from €47 for a return, depending on time of year and type of excursion. A modest fuel surcharge is also applicable.

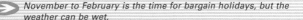

November to February is the time for bargain holidays, but the weather can be wet.

Left **Madeiran policeman** Right **Pharmacy**

TOP 10 Health and Security

1 Insurance
Make sure that you take out adequate travel insurance to cover yourself for private medical treatment, as well as for loss or theft of belongings. You should also be certain that your policy is valid for any holiday activities you might undertake, such as riding, scuba diving or water skiing. If you plan to hire a car while you are on the island, it might also be advisable to take out personal liability cover for damage to rented vehicles.

2 EHIC
If you are an EU citizen, you are entitled to claim free emergency medical treatment, but you must obtain a European Health Insurance Card (EHIC), either by filling in an application form, available from a post office, or by applying online. You usually have to pay for medical treatment in the first instance, then reclaim costs later, so retain receipts for any medical expenses that you incur.

3 Bites and Stings
Mosquitoes are not a major problem on the island, and there are no poisonous snakes or insects. Stray dogs and so-called "guard dogs" can be a hazard; some walkers carry dog dazers to protect themselves from unwanted attention. Treatment should be sought for dog bites, but there is no record of rabies on Madeira.

4 Sun Protection
It is easy to suffer sunburn on Madeira at any time of the year, especially as the effects of too much sun are not apparent until some time after exposure. Cover your head, neck, arms and legs if you are exposed to the sun, use sunscreen, and carry sufficient water to prevent dehydration.

5 Health Centres
If you do need medical help, you will receive both swift and attentive service by going to the nearest health centre – in Portuguese, Centro de Saúde. Such centres are found in every village and parish.

6 Pharmacies
Pharmacies – or *farmácias* – have staff trained to diagnose minor ailments and prescribe appropriate remedies. Every village has a late-opening pharmacy – and any pharmacies that do not open late will have a notice on the door directing you to one that does.

7 Spa Therapy
You don't have to be ill to benefit from the many spa therapies on offer in Madeira. This is especially true of Porto Santo, where all of the larger hotels have therapy centres offering hydrotherapy, aromatherapy, skincare, detox and massage treatments. Ask your hotel to give you a recommendation.

8 Crime
Madeira is still refreshingly safe and free from crime – including pick-pocketing, vandalism and generally antisocial behaviour. Even so, it would be unwise to tempt fate by being too careless; lock all your valuables in a hotel safe, or keep them close when out and about.

9 Police
If you lose any valuables, and intend to make an insurance claim, you will need to make an official police report. The main police station in Funchal is at Rua da Infância 28; the police telephone exchange can be reached on 291 208 400. There are police posts in every town.

10 Vehicle Breakdown
There is no national breakdown service on Madeira, but car rental companies will give you the emergency number of their own service.

Emergency Services

Fire, police and ambulance
112

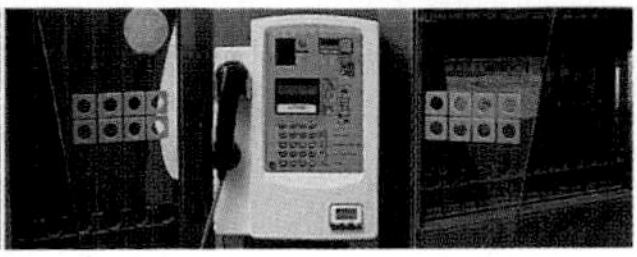

Left **Bank of Portugal** Right **Telephone kiosk**

TOP 10 Banking and Communications

1 Currency

Madeira uses the euro. Because of forgery, big notes tend to be treated with suspicion, so ask for a mix of €50, €20 and €10 notes when changing money.

2 Exchange

Banks in Madeira can be found in every town, and nearly all have an exchange service for which they charge a minimum fee no matter how large or small the transaction, so it is a good idea to change larger amounts at a time. Such charges apply to traveller's cheques, as well as transactions with cash. Take your passport with you when you change money. Banks open 8:30am–3pm Monday to Friday, though some also open on Saturday until 1pm.

3 Cash Machines

Nearly all banks also have a hole-in-the-wall cash machine *(multibanco)* that you can use to obtain euros using a card that is part of the Visa or MasterCard network and your PIN number. Such transactions may be subject to an administration fee and also interest payments charged by your own card company.

4 Credit Cards

Theoretically, credit cards are accepted in most shops, as well as the more upmarket restaurants, but most businesses prefer cash. As a result, you may be given the excuse that there is a problem with your card, or told that it is not compatible with the system in Madeira, which, for most cards, requires you to key a PIN number into a keypad.

5 Public Phones

Card-operated phones are found in most town and village centres. Cards can be purchased from most newsagents, as well as supermarkets, and offer the cheapest way of calling home. To phone abroad, dial the international access code (00) and the country code (UK 44, US 1), then the area code without the initial zero, and finally the actual number.

6 Mobile Phones

Mobile coverage on Madeira is good, but the dialling rules differ from network to network, so check with your service provider before you go what codes you need to use to call someone from Madeira or for someone to call you.

7 Post Offices

Every town has a post office *(correios)*. Funchal's most central post office is on Avenida Zarco (8:30am–8pm Mon–Fri, 9am–1pm Sat). Poste restante services are available at the main post office on Avenida Calouste Gulbenkian (same hours). Correspondence should be marked "Poste Restante", and you will need your passport to collect mail. Stamps can be purchased from most places that sell postcards.

8 Internet

Madeira is no stranger to cyberspace. Many hotels offer free webmail and internet access to their guests. Funchal has a number of Internet cafés offering fast connections, printers, café services and multilingual staff; they include Cyber Café, Global Net Café and BMF Internet.
Cyber Café: Avenida do Infante 6. Map Q1 • Esp@ço Internet: Praça do Município. Map P3 • BMF Internet: Monumental Lido Shopping Centre, shop 14. Map G6

9 Television

Most hotels subscribe to the standard package of 30 satellite channels available on Madeira, including programmes in most European languages, plus MTV, CNN and BBC World. Reception tends to be somewhat variable outside Funchal.

10 Newspapers

Most newsagents in Funchal stock copies of the international editions of the main European daily newspapers. *The Brit* is an English language publication.
www.thebrit.co.uk

The area code for Madeira and Porto Santo is 291. This number has to be dialled even when you are in Madeira or Porto Santo.

Left **Dolphin-watching yacht, Funchal** Right **Botanical Gardens, Funchal**

Top 10 Specialist Holidays

1 Fly/Drive

You can experience Madeira to the full by using rural hotels as bases for walks and tours. The leading operators are Atlantic Holidays and Sunvil in the UK; and Abreu Tours and Portugal Online in the US. *www.atlanticholidays.net • www.sunvil.co.uk • www.abreu-tours.com • www.portugal.com*

2 Walking

Booking yourself on an organized walking tour means that everything is done for you, including ferrying your luggage around – all you have to do is enjoy the scenery. *www.headwater.com • www.exodus.co.uk • www.discoverytravel.co.uk • www.responsibletravel.com • www.ramblersholidays.co.uk*

3 Parks and Gardens

Specialist holidays allow you to see some of Madeira's private gardens – rich depositories of rare plants – as well as visiting public gardens with an expert. *www.beautifulgardenholidays.co.uk*

4 Golf Packages

The Porto Bay Serra Golf *(see p115)* and the Casa Velha do Palheiro *(see p113)* both offer golf packages with discounted green fees, guaranteed tee times, clinics and one-to-one lessons at all levels. If your partner does not play, both hotels are well placed for visiting gardens and *levadas*.

5 Wildlife

From kiosks at Funchal's marina, several yacht charter companies organize wildlife and marine life expeditions, including dolphin- and whale-watching trips. *Bonita da Madeira: 291 762 218 • Ventura do Mar: 291 280 033 • Madeira Catamaran: 291 224 900 • Gavião Madeira: 291 241 124*

6 Fishing

Madeira's waters teem with big-game fish, including blue and white marlin, big-eye and bluefin tuna, albacore and bonito. Nautisantos, based at Funchal's marina, offers full- and half-day trips with equipment provided. It is a signatory to the tag-and-release scheme, whereby fish, once caught and photographed, are returned to the wild. *Nautisantos: 291 231 312; www.nautisantosfishing.com*

7 Diving

Just under the surface along Madeira's southern cliffs is a protected world of marine caves, colourful fish and crabs, sea urchins, corals and weeds that are invisible unless you know how to dive. Two hotels have permanent diving schools: Manta Diving is at the Galomar *(see p115)* in Caniço de Baixo and Madeira Oceanos is at Dom Pedro Baía Club in Machico. *Manta Diving: www.mantadiving.com • Focus Natura: 916 409 780; www.focusnatura.com*

8 Adventure

Madeira is the ideal destination for a range of adventure sports, from mountain biking and rock climbing to windsurfing, canyoning and paragliding. *Terras de Aventura: 291 708 990; www.terrasdeaventura.com*

9 Spa Holidays

Several hotels have large spa complexes. These include the Choupana Hills Resort and Spa *(see p113)*, the Atlantic Sea Spa at the Vidamar Resort *(see p112)*, the Vital Centre at the Jardim Atlântico *(see p116)*, the Divine Spa at The Vine *(see p112)*, the Spa at the Porto Mare *(see p112)* and the Spa at the Pestana Porto Santo *(see p99)*.

10 Honeymoons and Romantic Breaks

Many of Madeira's graceful old manor house hotels reserve their finest rooms for honeymooners, or those celebrating a special anniversary. The island's scenery and sunsets, as well as its indulgent pool and spa complexes, make for a memorable holiday. *www.classic-collection.co.uk • www.prestigeholidays.co.uk*

Left **Walking along the Levada do Risco** Right **Madeiran bus**

TOP 10 Walking Tips

1 Give it a Go

Many walkers rate Madeira as one of the most rewarding European destinations and visit the island regularly. Find out why walking on Madeira can be so addictive by trying a short walk on your own, or by signing up for a guided walking tour *(see p51)*.

2 Maps and Guides

Madeira is changing so fast that no map or guide is fully up-to-date. Users of Sunflower Books' *Madeira* walking guide are extremely good at providing feedback on the latest changes, which are posted on the publisher's website. *www.sunflowerbooks.co.uk*

3 Mountains or Woods

Everyone likes variety, but there are those who opt for mountain walks and others who prefer a woodland stroll. Madeira caters to both, with steep cobbled paths linking the peaks of the island's central mountain range, where vegetation is sparse, and *levada* paths that follow the contours through more gentle, domesticated landscapes.

4 Be Prepared

Check a reliable guide to see what hazards you can expect on the route and prepare accordingly. Mountain walks lack shade and are susceptible to sudden downpours or clouds that obscure the way ahead. *Levada* walks can be muddy and may involve long tunnels, waterfalls that cascade over the path or streams that have to be waded.

5 Choosing a Base

If you have come to Madeira just to walk, Funchal might not be the best place to stay. You may prefer to choose a hotel that is closer to a good choice of routes, such as the Pousada dos Vinháticos *(see p116)*, the Hotel Encumeada *(see p116)* or the Solar de Boaventura *(see p115)*.

6 Cars and Taxis

There are very few circular walks on Madeira. Fortunately, you can arrange to be dropped off and collected by taxi, or you can call a cab once you reach the end of your walk. Another option is to drive to the starting point of your walk, and take a taxi back to your car at the end.

7 Buses

A good walking guide will provide details of bus connections as well as a timing guide, so that you can see in advance how long each route will take. Madeira's rural buses are reliable, but on long-distance routes across the island, there is only one bus a day, so you might have to get to the start of the walk by bus and return by taxi, or vice versa.

8 Mobile Phones

Mobile phones can be a pest, but they may also be a life-saver when used to call for help in an emergency. They are also useful simply for letting your taxi driver know how long you will be. If you do not have a mobile phone, let your hotel know where you are going and at what time you are due back, so that someone can raise the alarm if you fail to return.

9 Field Guide

Nothing can be more annoying than not being able to put a name to all the flowers, ferns, succulents and lichens that you will see along the route. Consider investing in a wildlife guide, such as *Madeira's Natural History in a Nutshell* by Peter Sziemer, available at most Funchal bookshops *(see p57)*. Rather heavier than its title implies, it will tell you all you need to know about the island's geology, flora and fauna.

10 Picnics

Don't forget to pack a picnic to enjoy in a sunny glade or at a panoramic viewing point along your route. Any leftover crumbs of bread can be fed to the birds that will come to see what you are up to, or to the trout (escapees from local trout farms) that you may spot in some of the island's rivers and *levadas*.

Left **Royal Savoy pool complex** Right **View from Quinta Bela de São Tiago**

Top 10 Accommodation Tips

1 Price and Location
On Madeira, location has a big influence on price. City-centre hotels tend to be cheap. The luxurious five-star hotels with sea views, along the Estrada Monumental to the west of the city, command the highest prices. Further west, in the hotel zone, prices fall the further you go from the city centre and from the sea.

2 A Room with a View
Some hotels have been designed so that every room looks out over the sea. Where this is not the case, you will find that you pay significantly more for a room with a sea view, especially if it has a sunny, south-facing balcony.

3 Beware of Noise
If you are sensitive to noise, make sure that you tell the hotel. Some rooms with so-called "mountain views" actually look out onto one of the island's busiest roads, the Estrada Monumental. You may also have trouble with noise if your room is located above the hotel restaurant, especially if it has live music or a disco.

4 Grading Systems
Madeira's grading system is a fairly accurate guide to the facilities you can expect. All four- and five-star (and most three-star) hotels offer heating, air conditioning, television, direct-dial telephone, a garage or parking facilities, a restaurant and a bar. The star grading system is not, however, a measure of service, ambience, character or quality.

5 Quintas and Estalagens
Estalagens (inns) or *quintas* (manor houses) are usually hotels of some age and historic character, often set on an estate with mature trees and fine gardens. In most cases, the bar, dining room and lounges are located in the old house, while guest rooms may be in modern blocks in the grounds.

6 Rural Tourism and Country Hotels
Farmers and landowners on Madeira are being encouraged to convert redundant agricultural buildings into cottages. To find one, look for green signs with the words *Turismo Rural*, ask at local tourist offices or check out Madeira's rural tourism website, through which you can book some 20 such properties around the island.
www.madeirarural.com

7 Children
Most hotel rooms are designed for double occupancy, but you are welcome to ask for an extra bed or two for children. Some hotels have family rooms that sleep four to six people.

8 Peak Seasons
Madeira is popular with Portuguese escaping the summer heat of the mainland, so hotels tend to be busy during July and August, when it is best to book well ahead. Other popular times are Christmas and New Year, the Carnival and Flower Festival, and the weeks before, during and after Easter. At all these times, room rates can be double the norm.

9 Winter Breaks
You can secure some exceptional bargains by visiting Madeira between November and February, when even Belmond Reid's Palace has been known to offer discounts. Look out for offers in newspaper supplements, or check with Madeira specialists.
Madeira Hotel Guide: www.madeira-portugal.com
• *www.atlanticholidays.net*
• *www.saga.co.uk*
• *www.thomson.co.uk*

10 Breakfast and Half-Board
Hotel prices on Madeira usually include a buffet breakfast (cereals, fresh fruit, juices, pastries, cooked meats, cheese, tea and coffee). Cooked breakfast is an option at deluxe hotels. Opting for half-board, with dinner in the hotel restaurant, can be good value, though your choice may be limited to just two dishes per course, rather than the full à la carte menu.

Left **Expensive taxis** Right **Charter flight at Madeira airport**

TOP 10 Madeira on a Budget

1 Book Ahead and Online
Madeira can be very cheap, even more so now that several "no-frills" carriers such as Jet2, Thomsonfly and easyJet serve the island. Scheduled flights are rarely discounted, due to the high demand. The best way to secure a discount is to book at least three months in advance, using an online agent such as Expedia.

2 Be Flexible
The best discounts are had by those who are flexible about their travel dates and don't mind flying early in the morning or late at night. Online agents show seat costs for different flights and allow you to choose the cheapest. The downside is that, once booked, discounted tickets cannot be changed without paying a hefty penalty.

3 Charter Flights
UK charter airlines such as Airtours, Jet2, Thomsonfly and easyJet can offer the cheapest way to get to Madeira, but many of them only offer flights here between April and October. They may only fly once a week, so a short break is not an option.

4 Packages
Madeira's hotels are often not responsive to requests for a room discount, even when they are quiet. The best way to secure a cheap deal is to book an all inclusive package (including flights, room, meals, transfers, car hire and excursions) online or through an agent.

5 Last-minute Bargains
If you can travel at a week or two's notice, check travel agents' windows and advertised last-minute bargains. In some cases, you will not know where you are staying until you arrive, but bad hotels are rare on Madeira (and noise nuisance is more likely than a safety or hygiene problem).

6 Accommodation
Madeira has some astonishingly cheap accommodation in the city centre and at rural *pensions (see p117).* Clean rooms with a shared bathroom are available for €15 to €25 a night, and even luxurious apartments can be had for €45 a night, if you are staying for a week or more. www.madeira-island.com has a useful accommodation section, which has links to the websites of several of Madeira's cheaper hotels.

7 Food
Madeira has literally hundreds of cheap cafés and restaurants, where you can eat very well for €10 a head by choosing simple dishes, such as grilled sardines and salad. Better still, shop in local markets and supermarkets. Delicious bread, olives, fresh fruit and salad ingredients are all inexpensive, as well as ready-cooked dishes such as grilled chicken or beef-and-bean stew.

8 Transport
Avoid taxis and you will save money. You may have to wait up to an hour for the airport bus into Funchal, but it costs a few euros, compared with a minimum taxi fare of €30 one way. Use public transport to travel around the island and take advantage of hotel courtesy buses. It is worth haggling over the price of island taxi tours.

9 Guided Tours
Guided tours offer another cost-saving alternative to taxis or car hire. The downside is that you may be obliged to travel in a large group of people, and the trip may well include shop and restaurant stops that you might not want to make. *www.lido-tours.com*

10 Bars and Entertainment
You can easily save money by avoiding discos and other nightlife venues where prices for drinks are much higher than in ordinary bars. In the same way, drinking in local bars is cheaper than in hotel bars.

Left **Flower stall** Right **Vintage Madeira wine**

TOP 10 Shopping Tips

1 Duty Free

Prices in Madeira airport's duty free shop are generally more expensive than in downtown wine shops and supermarkets. However, non-EU residents are entitled to a VAT refund.

2 Embroidery

Make sure that you don't pay high prices for cheap, machine-made embroidery imported from Asia, if what you are after is the genuine local article. All Madeiran embroidery is checked for quality before being passed for sale. It is marked with a hologram tag – and in some cases by a lead seal.

3 Non-vintage Wines

If you want to taste and buy quality Madeira wine *(see p59)*, make sure the label mentions Sercial, Verdelho, Bual or Malvasia. This shows that the wine is of high quality and made by traditional methods, using the classic grape varieties. Wines labelled dry, medium dry, medium sweet or rich are mass-produced and lack the subtlety and complexity of the best Madeira.

4 Aguardente

Another souvenir with a long history is *aguardente* (sugar cane spirit), often described as "rum". White *aguardente* lacks subtlety and is commonly served as *poncha*, mixed with lemon and honey. Aged, dark *aguardente* is a different matter entirely – an after-dinner drink with real character and flavour.

5 Leather Bargains

Prices on Madeira are generally higher than those found elsewhere in Europe because of the cost of importing goods to the island. The two exceptions to this rule are shoes and leather goods, which are Portuguese specialities. There are plenty of leather shops to browse in along the narrow streets around the cathedral in Funchal *(see p57)*.

6 Flowers

To make sure that your flowers are as fresh as possible, and that they survive the journey home, ask the florist to deliver them to your hotel on the morning of your departure, packed in a robust cardboard container. Beware, however, that these boxes may be regarded as hold luggage if they exceed the maximum dimensions allowed for hand baggage, and hence, will attract an excess charge. The best thing to do is to check with your carrier before purchasing flowers.

7 Bolo de Mel

Another popular and long-lasting choice of souvenir is Madeiran Christmas cake, now made and sold all year round. Called *bolo de mel* (honey cake), it is a traditional cake made to a recipe that includes sugar cane syrup and spices and is an excellent teatime treat.

8 Shopping Centres

Though they are threatening to drive the island's small shopkeepers out of business, there is no doubt that for sheer choice and variety, the best places to shop in Funchal are the large shopping centres. Among the main ones are Dolce Vita Shopping *(see p69)* and Madeira Shopping *(see p69)*. Another huge mall, Forum Madeira *(see p69)*, is located in the hotel zone.

9 Supermarkets

Large supermarkets can also be good for souvenir hunting. Try the one at the Anadia Centre, opposite the Farmers' Market in Funchal, or the one at the Lido, in the centre of the hotel zone. The supermarket chain *Pingo Doce* is also worth trying.

10 Scrimshaws

A word of warning: you may see carved whalebone ivory for sale in Caniçal and in other parts of the island. The trade is a relic of the days when this region of Madeira had a whaling fleet. Do not be tempted to buy: taking whalebone products out of the country is illegal.

Left **Unofficial tourist information centre** Right **Trawling for custom outside of a restaurant**

Top 10 Things to Avoid

1 Taxi Fares

Taxis operate on the meter as well as off it. Fare for popular routes such as the journey to and from the airport, is fixed. Taxi drivers are legally obliged to display a table of fixed fares, but can use their meters for other journeys, unless you have agreed a price in advance. Aitram Taxis sell fixed-fare vouchers for several island sightseeing excursions.

2 Timeshare Touts

The problem is not as bad as in some other holiday resorts, but timeshare touts do operate in Funchal, accosting people on Avenida do Infante as they stroll into downtown Funchal from the hotel zone. If somebody greets you with a cheery "Hello, do you speak English?", there's a good chance that he's a tout. They are not very persistent, so just answer with a polite "No, thank you".

3 Restaurant Touts

Restaurant touts are more difficult to shake off than the timeshare variety. They operate especially in the Zone Velha (Old Town), the marina complex and the restaurant strip along Caminho da Casa Branca. If you want to browse menus before choosing where to eat, it is best to do this in the morning or afternoon, avoiding times when restaurants trawl for customers.

4 Lobster

Remember that the oh-so-tempting "fresh lobster" much touted in seafood restaurants could end up costing you a small fortune. Lobsters are imported and priced by weight, so make sure you know exactly how much you will be charged.

5 Information Centres

Various establishments along the route from the hotel zone to downtown Funchal call themselves "tourist information centres" and offer free maps. In reality, they are tour agents that will extol the delights of Madeira in order to sign you up on a guided tour.

6 Guided Tours

Scores of tour companies offer identical trips in air-conditioned coaches. These are a good way of getting a quick overview of Madeira, but they involve compulsory shopping and restaurant stops. To gain a more personal view of the island, choose a mini-bus tour or ask your hotel to recommend a taxi driver who speaks English.

7 Aggressive Drivers

If you are thinking of hiring a taxi for a day or half-day trip, make sure the driver knows that fast driving and daredevil overtaking do not impress you. Aggressive driving is particularly dangerous on Madeira's narrow, twisting roads; it also leads to car sickness.

8 Hidden Car Costs

If you decide to hire a car and want to compare prices, don't be guided by the advertised daily rates. Make sure there are no hidden extras, such as tax and insurance, which can add 20 per cent or more to the basic daily rate.

9 Out-of-date Maps

Once you have your car, you might well want a map or a walking guide. Beware: most of the maps and guides sold in souvenir shops are years out of date, and can be seriously misleading, given how much Madeira has developed in recent years. Choose a reliable bookshop *(see p57)* and check the publication date before you buy.

10 Swimming

Madeira's waters are among the cleanest in Europe. However, the Atlantic Ocean can be unpredictable and strong currents are natural hazards at many points along the coast. A red flag flying over a beach forbids bathers from entering the sea, while a green flag means it is safe to swim. If a yellow flag is hoisted, then bathers may remain at the water's edge but should not go swimming.

Left **Belmond Reid's Palace interior** Right **Quinta da Casa Branca**

TOP 10 Character Hotels in Funchal

1 Belmond Reid's Palace

One of the great hotels of the world, Reid's has the feel of a country house – genuine antiques and works of art at every turn, gardens dotted with pools and shady retreats, panoramic views, and some of Madeira's best restaurants *(see p60)*. *Estrada Monumental 139 • Map H6 • 291 717 171 • www.reidspalace.com • €€€€€*

2 The Vine

The epitome of style and sophistication, this urban retreat, with its stunning interiors, offers deluxe rooms and suites. Madeira wine massage and red wine bath options are available in the spa. A plunge pool, bar and the Uva gourmet restaurant *(see p60)* crown the roof. *Rua dos Aranhas 27 • Map P2 • 291 009 000 • www.hotelthevine.com • €€€*

3 Royal Savoy

The modern Savoy is a veritable museum of art and antiquities from all the countries that Portuguese sailors ventured to during the 15th-century Age of Discovery. But the hotel's popularity with readers of the British *Daily Telegraph* has more to do with its stunningly designed pool area, and the delicious cocktails at the submerged bar. *Rua Carvalho Araújo • Map H6 • 291 213 500 • www.hotelroyalsavoymadeira.com • €€€€€*

4 Vidamar Resort Madeira

Natural light floods this elegant hotel's huge central atrium bedecked with modern artwork. A glorious seafront location, top-notch spa and four infinity pools are further enticements. *Estrada Monumental 175/177 • Map G6 • 291 717 600 • www.vidamarresorts.com • €€€€*

5 Cliff Bay

This fabulous oceanfront property is surrounded by terraced gardens that lead to palm-shaded swimming pools. It also has an excellent spa and a Michelin restaurant, Il Gallo d' Oro *(see p60)*. *Estrada Monumental 147 • Map G6 • 291 707 700 • www.portobay.com • €€€€*

6 Porto Mare

Centrepiece of the Vila Porto Mare resort, this captivating hotel stands in subtropical gardens that display 470 unique botanical species. Four restaurants, five pools, a spa complex, sports and children's facilities enhance the guest experience. *Rua Simplício Passos Gouveia 21 • Map G6 • 291 703 700 • www.portobay.com • €€€*

7 Madeira Regency Palace

Colonial-style architecture provides this hotel with a charming ambiance. Leisure facilities include the Mango Health Club & Spa plus swimming pools amidst subtropical flora. All rooms offer stunning sea views. *Estrada Monumental 275 • Map G6 • 291 703 000 • www.madeiraregencypalace.com • €€€*

8 Quinta da Casa Branca

The ultra-modern rooms in this imaginatively designed complex are cleverly integrated into the garden so as to be almost invisible, while providing guests with uninterrupted views across green lawns and shrub-filled borders. Note that the hotel has a minimum stay policy. *Rua da Casa Branca 5/7 • Map G6 • 291 700 770 • www.quintacasabranca.pt • €€€€€*

9 Quinta da Penha de França

This charming hotel is the best central budget choice. The busy world only intrudes when using the footbridge to access the pool and sea platform. *Rua Imperatriz Dona Amélia 87 • Map H6 • 291 204 650 • www.penhafranca.com • €€*

10 Pestana Grand

This spacious hotel has a large outdoor pool and health centre. Eat Portuguese, Italian or Moroccan before enjoying the evening's entertainment. *Rua Ponta da Cruz 23 • Map G6 • 291 707 400 • www.pestana.com • €€€*

Note: *Unless otherwise stated, all hotels accept credit cards, and have en-suite bathrooms and air conditioning*

Choupana Hills Resort

Price Categories

For a standard, double room per night (with breakfast if included), taxes and extra charges.	€ under €50
	€€ €50–100
	€€€ €100–150
	€€€€ €150–200
	€€€€€ over €200

TOP 10 Character Hotels beyond Funchal

1 Choupana Hills Resort and Spa, Funchal

A stunning complex of bungalows of wood, stone and tile, high up in the menthol-scented eucalyptus forest above Funchal. Enjoy a few days of pampering – complete with massage and spa treatments, and a fine restaurant, the Xôpana *(see p61)*. *Travessa do Largo da Choupana • Map H5 • 291 206 020 • www.choupanahills.com • €€€€*

2 Casa Velha do Palheiro, São Gonçalo

The 200-year-old Casa Velha serves some of the best food on the island *(see p61)*. The Palheiro Gardens *(see pp24–5)* are just over the hedge; Palheiro Golf *(see p48)* is at the end of the drive. It also offers modern spa facilities. *Rua da Estalagem 23 • Map H5 • 291 790 350 • www.casa-velha.com • €€€€*

3 Quinta do Monte, Monte

An oasis of calm, set high above Funchal in a lush, walled garden threaded by meandering cobbled paths. The manor at the heart of the estate is decorated with antique furniture and oriental rugs. The dining room is set in a modern conservatory. *Caminho do Monte 182 • Map H5 • 291 780 100 • www.charminghotelsmadeira.com • €€€*

4 Madeira Regency Cliff, Funchal

Located in the fashionable Lido district, this hotel combines modern decor, a lively colour scheme and clever use of ambient light. All rooms and suites overlook Funchal Bay, as does the Mistral restaurant-bar. Luxuries include the Oceanus Health Club and outdoor pools. *Travessa Quinta Calaça 6 • Map G6 • 291 710 700 • www.regencycliff.com • €€€*

5 Quinta Splendida, Caniço

Tucked away in botanical gardens that feature over 1,000 rare plant species, this 19th century restored manor has 141 rooms, 25 spa suites and three restaurants. The Quinta's spa is one of the largest in Madeira. *Estrada da Ponta Oliveira 11 • Map J5 • 291 930 400 • www.quintasplendida.com • €€€€*

6 Quinta da Bela Vista, Funchal

The "Beautiful View" is of the wild cliffs to the east, but it could equally be describing the lovely gardens of this traditional manor house. *Caminho do Avista Navios 4 • Map G6 • 291 706 400 • www.belavistamadeira.com • €€€€*

7 Jardins do Lago, Funchal

This charming manor house, set in verdant gardens, once hosted General Beresford during the Napoleonic wars. Rooms enjoy southerly views over the city. Features include a pool, tennis court, spa suite, billiards room and restaurant. *Rua Dr João Lemos Gomes 29 • Map H5 • 291 750 100 • www.jardinsdolago.com • €€€*

8 Quintinha de São João, Funchal

Set in an elegant suburb of Funchal, the Quintinha de São João has modern wings extending from its historic core. Facilities include outdoor pool, tennis court, spa, sauna and well regarded restaurant. *Rua da Levada de São João 4 • Map H5 • 291 740 920 • www.quintinhasaojoao.com • €€€*

9 Quinta Mirabela, Funchal

Built in 1888, this is now a delightfully chic country inn with luxurious rooms and suites. The view is reason enough to stay, but so too are the cuisine, health club and terrace pool. *Caminho do Monte 105/107 • Map H5 • 291 780 210 • www.quinta-mirabela.com • €€€*

10 Quinta das Vistas, Funchal

This 1930s-style hotel set high above the city has something of a colonial air, with palm-fringed public rooms and gardens. Pool, gym, spa and a gourmet restaurant. *Caminho de Santo António 52 • Map G5 • 291 750 007 • www.charming-hotels-madeira.com • €€€*

For hotels on Porto Santo **See p99**

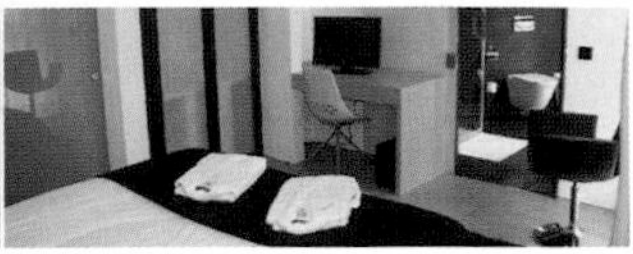

Left **Quinta Bela São Tiago room** Right **Funchal Design Hotel**

Top 10 City-centre Hotels in Funchal

1 Quinta Bela São Tiago

Birdsong and tranquil gardens make you wonder whether you really are just a five-minute stroll from the busy heart of Funchal. Rooms – some of them huge – have views of the onion-domed church towers and terracotta roofs of the Zona Velha (Old Town). Outdoor pool and gym. *Rua Bela de São Tiago 70 • Map P6 • 291 204 500 • www.quintabelasaotiago.com • €€€*

2 Porto Santa Maria

Built on the site of the city's former shipyard, the hotel overlooks Funchal's seafront promenade and is centrally located for shopping and restaurants. It has two pools and a rooftop jacuzzi. *Avenida do Mar 50 • Map Q5 • 291 206 700 • www.portobay.com • €€€€*

3 Quinta Perestrello

Set in mature gardens, this heritage hotel is a fine example of the elegant houses built by Madeiran merchants. Most of the rooms are in the old building – those at the back are quietest. Swimming pool. *Rua do Dr Pita 3 • Map G6 • 291 706 700 • www.charming-hotels-madeira.com • €€€*

4 Pestana Casino Park

If you want nightlife and entertainment, a stay at this huge 1960s hotel is as good as it gets, with a full programme of dinner dances and professional cabaret. The Copacabana Nightclub and the Madeira Casino are part of the complex. Gym, sauna, pool, tennis courts. *Rua Imperatriz Dona Amélia 55 • Map Q1 • 291 209 100 • www.pestana.com • €€€*

5 Enotel Quinta do Sol

The Enotel Quinta do Sol is next to a busy road, but it has rooms overlooking the quiet green gardens of the Quinta Magnólia to the rear, or the hotel's own pool terrace. Many guests return – a credit to the friendliness of the staff. Live music and folklore performances. *Rua do Dr Pita 6 • Map H6 • 291 707 010 • www.enotelquintadosol.com • €€*

6 Funchal Design Hotel

Converted from a private residence, this funky, child-friendly boutique hotel surprises with its sleek, minimalist decor and two-tone colour scheme. Rooms include a kitchenette with electric cooker and microwave; there's also a restaurant. *Rua da Alegria 2–2A • Map P1 • 291 780 210 • www.funchaldesignhotel.com • €€€*

7 Residencial Gordon

Located in a backstreet near the English Church *(see p42)*, this plainly decorated hotel is a wonderful retreat for no-frills travellers. There's an appealing sun terrace at the rear, and private parking. Staff speak basic English. *Rua do Quebra Costas 34 • Map N1 • 291 742 366 • www.residencial-gordon.com • €*

8 Albergaria Catedral

Original 1970s furniture lends this guesthouse a delightfully retro feel. Located in the heart of the city, the cosmopolitan atmosphere is tangible. Breakfast can be enjoyed on a panoramic terrace overlooking the cathedral. *Rua do Aljube 13 • Map P3 • 291 230 091 • www.albergariacatedral.com • €€*

9 Residencial da Mariazinha

Located on Funchal's oldest street, which is beautifully cobbled and buzzing with life, this hotel is a smart residence with nine spacious rooms and a suite with its own jacuzzi. *Rua de Santa Maria 155 • Map P5 • 291 220 239 • www.residencialmariazinha.com • €*

10 Pestana Carlton Madeira

This big tower block behind the Savoy wins no prize for architecture, but its garden and pool complex is equal to those at any of the nearby luxury hotels. Opposite Belmond Reid's Palace, it offers similar views for a lot less euros. *Largo António Nobre • Map H6 • 291 239 500 • www.pestana.com • €€€€*

***Note:** Unless otherwise stated, all hotels accept credit cards, and have ensuite bathrooms and air conditioning*

Royal Orchid Hotel, Caniço de Baixo

Price Categories

For a standard, double room per night (with breakfast if included), taxes and extra charges.

€	under €50
€€	€50–100
€€€	€100–150
€€€€	€150–200
€€€€€	over €200

Top 10 Hotels in the East of the Island

1 Four Views Oasis, Caniço de Baixo

This large resort in Caniço's hotel district, has a gym, sauna, jacuzzi, indoor and outdoor pools and courtesy bus. *Praia dos Reis Magos • Map J6 • 291 930 100 • www.fourviewshotels.com • €€*

2 Royal Orchid, Caniço de Baixo

One of Caniço's many luxury hotels, the Royal Orchid has almost everything you could want in a resort hotel. All rooms have a kitchenette and some have seaview balconies. *Travessa Vista da Praia • Map J6 • 291 934 600 • www.hotelroyalorchid.com • €€€*

3 White Waters, Machico

Located close to the airport, this family-run boutique hotel with contemporary architecture, has rooms overlooking the beautiful sea. Guests can dine at the restaurant or unwind in the tea garden on the terrace. Machico's sandy beach *(see p46)* is at a short distance. *Praceta 25 de Abril • Map K4 • 291 969 380 • www.whitewaters-madeira.com • €€*

4 Galomar, Caniço de Baixo

An elevator links the main hotel to an extensive lido at the base of Caniço's towering cliffs. The lido is home to the Manta Diving School, so a fair proportion of guests choose the hotel in order to be able to dive in the rich marine reserve that surrounds the lido. *Ponta da Oliveira • Map J6 • 291 930 930 • www.galoresort.com • €€*

5 Porto Bay Serra Golf, Santo de Serra

A short walk from the prestigious Santo da Serra Golf Course, this charming property offers luxuries such as a traditional restaurant, covered pool, spa, library, games room and gym. *Sítio dos Casais Próximos • Map J4 • 291 550 500 • www.portobay.com • €€*

6 Estalagem do Santo, Santo António da Serra

This country inn with indoor pool, tennis court and pretty gardens makes a good base for exploring the east of the island. It's also close to the golf course at Santo da Serra. *Casais Próximos • Map J4 • 291 550 550 • www.enotel.com • €€*

7 Quinta do Furão, Santana

Rooms at this luxurious modern hotel enjoy breathtaking views along the rugged north coast of Madeira. Built on a headland just on the edge of Santana, the hotel is surrounded by the vineyards of the Madeira Wine Company. A bonus for guests is the chance to tour the vineyards, and even help with the harvest if it's that time of year. Heated outdoor pool, sauna and gym. *Estrada Quinta do Furão 6 • Map H2 • 291 570 100 • www.quintadofurao.com • €€€*

8 Cabanas de São Jorge, São Jorge

The *cabanas*, or "cabins", are South African-style *rondhovels* ("round houses") set in peaceful gardens with dizzying clifftop views. This is an excellent place to break your journey and get to know the north coast. *Beira da Quinta • Map H2 • 291 576 356 • www.cabanasvillage.com • €€*

9 Solar de Boaventura, Boaventura

Tastefully converted from a classic Madeiran house dating back to 1776. The rooms are large. The restaurant serves local specialities. *Serrão Boaventura • Map G2 • 291 860 888 • www.solar-boaventura.com • €€*

10 Albatroz Beach & Yacht Club, Santa Cruz

Enjoying relative seclusion right on the seafront, this is a great place for relaxation. All rooms have balconies with ocean views. Facilities include a pool. *Quinta Dr Américo Durão, Sítio da Terça • Map K5 • 291 520 290 • www.albatrozhotel.com • €€€*

Left **Jardim Atlântico** Right **Quinta do Alto de São João**

TOP 10 Hotels in the West of the Island

1 Quinta do Estreito, Câmara de Lobos

This was once the main wine estate in the area. The old house is now the setting for the Bacchus gourmet restaurant and the Vintage bar and library; the old wine lodge now houses the Adega da Quinta restaurant *(see p79)*. Modern guest quarters are set in landscaped gardens with an olive grove and organic vegetable plot. *Rua José Joaquim da Costa • Map F6 • 291 910 530 • www.charminghotelsmadeira.com • €€*

2 Estalagem da Ponta do Sol, Ponta do Sol

Enjoy views of the setting sun from this stylish clifftop hotel. Distinctive bridges and towers link modern guest quarters with the more traditional bar and library area and the glass-walled restaurant. Leisure facilities include a spa, pool and panoramic jacuzzi. *Quinta da Rochinha • Map D5 • 291 970 200 • www.pontadosol.com • €€*

3 Enotel Baia, Ponta do Sol

This hotel, which cleverly retains all the old façades that have graced the palm-lined esplanade since the 19th century, is an ideal family break option. Baby-sitting services available. *Avenida 10 de Maio • Map D5 • 291 970 140 • www.enotel.com • €€*

4 Quinta do Alto de São João, Ponta do Sol

Open your window and hear nothing but the bees in the gardens. With a set daily menu and attentive staff, you will feel like a guest in the home of an absent aristocrat. *Lomba de São João • Map D5 • 291 222 667 • www.madeiramanorhotel.com • €*

5 Jardim Atlântico, Prazeres

The remoteness of this hotel is part of its charm. Guests are encouraged to explore the surrounding coast and countryside. Rooms, complete with kitchens, are huge. There is a mini-market on site. *Lombo da Rocha • Map B3 • 291 820 220 • www.jardimatlantico.com • €€€*

6 Pousada dos Vinháticos, Serra de Água

This small country inn sits on a saddle of rock between two of the island's most majestic groups of mountains. There is no better way to end the day than with drinks on the hotel terrace as the setting sun lights up the west-facing peaks. *Map E4 • 291 952 344 • www.pousadadosvinhaticos.com • €€*

7 Residencial Encumeada, Serra de Água

A little higher up the valley than the Pousada dos Vinháticos, this modern hotel boasts fine views. Surrounded by natural laurel forest, it is close to some of the best *levada* and mountain paths that the island has to offer. *Feiteiras • Map E4 • 291 951 282 • www.hotelencumeada.com • €*

8 Estalagem Eira do Serrado, Eira do Serrado

The northern façade of this small mountain hotel consists of glass, so that diners in the restaurant and guests in the rooms can enjoy the spectacular views of the Curral das Freiras and its encircling cliffs *(see p30)*. *Map G4 • 291 710 060 • www.eiradoserrado.com • €*

9 Pensão Salgueiro, Porto Moniz

Known for its charming ambience and first-rate service, this friendly hotel serves traditional Madeiran cuisine. Some rooms have kitchenettes and offer great sea views. *Lugar do Tenente 34 • Map C1 • 291 850 080 • www.pensaosalgueiro.com • €*

10 Paúl do Mar Aparthotel, Paúl do Mar

This eco-friendly hotel makes a useful base for exploring the western coast. It has a pool and wellness centre offering oriental therapies. *Avenida dos Pescadores, Paulenses 168 • Map A3 • 291 870 050 • www.hotelpauldomar.com • €€*

Note: Unless otherwise stated, all hotels accept credit cards, and have en suite bathrooms and air conditioning

Avenue Park self-catering apartments

Price Categories

For a standard, double room per night (with breakfast if included), taxes and extra charges.

€	under €50
€€	€50–100
€€€	€100–150
€€€€	€150–200
€€€€€	over €200

TOP 10 Self-catering and Budget Hotels

1 Suite Hotel Eden Mar, Funchal

The Eden Mar offers good-value self-catering in well-furnished rooms with small kitchens. It also provides access to one of Madeira's best resort complexes, the Porto Mare *(see p112)*. *Rua do Gorgulho 2 • Map G6 • 291 709 700 • www.portobay.com • €€€*

2 Four Views Monumental Lido, Funchal

The well-priced rooms at this apartment hotel in the Hotel Zone have separate kitchens and living areas; bedrooms face onto a quiet inner atrium. Shops and the Lido are nearby. *Estrada Monumental 284 • Map G6 • 291 724 000 • www.fourviewshotels.com • €€*

3 Avenue Park, Funchal

The spacious, light and well-furnished apartment rooms at this self-catering establishment close to the centre of downtown Funchal are a real bargain. The private covered parking is a bonus. *Avda do Infante 26D • Map Q1 • 291 205 630 • www.avenuepark-madeira.com • €€*

4 Pensão Residencial Vila Teresinha, Funchal

Special deals abound at this delightful guesthouse near the Museu da Quinta das Cruzes *(see p14)*. The longer the stay, the lower the daily room rate, which includes breakfast. *Rua das Cruzes 21 • Map N1 • 291 741 723 • www.vilateresinha.com • €*

5 Rental Agencies

Several websites carry links to self-catering accommodation – apartments and villas – for rent by the week, or longer. Madeira Island Direct and Madeira Island are two of the most popular. Most concentrate on Funchal but other locations are represented. *www.madeiraislanddirect.com • www.madeira-island.com • www.torresforumplus.com • www.palheirorentals.com • www.holidaylettings.co.uk*

6 Bed-and-breakfast

English-style bed-and-breakfast has been taken to Madeira by Trevor and June Franks. Trejuno, their guesthouse, is midway between Funchal and Monte. Walking tips, free airport pickup, and inside information. *Estrada do Livramento 94 • Map H5 • 291 783 268 • www.tjwalking-madeira.com • €*

7 Camping

Officially, camping is illegal on Madeira, except at two designated sites – Porto Moniz and Porto Santo. Advance booking is advisable in July and August. *Porto Moniz tourist office: 291 853 075 • Porto Santo campsite: 291 982 160 • www.madeira-camping.com • €*

8 Budget Accommodation in Funchal

The following are clean, quiet and cheap *pensões, residenciais* and hotels in the heart of town. *Astória: Rua de João Gago 10; Map P3; 291 223 820; € • do Centro: Rua do Carmo 20; Map P4; 291 200 510; € • Chafariz: Rua do Estanco Velho 3; Map P3; 291 232 260; € • Sirius: Rua das Hortas 35; Map N4; 291 226 117; € • Residencial Zarco: Rua da Alfândega 113; Map P3; 291 223 716; €*

9 Budget Accommodation Outside of Funchal

The Hortensia Gardens *(see p79)* offers inexpensive accommodation within its peaceful gardens.The family-run Residencial Prisma has 14 double and single rooms. At O Escondidinho das Canas in Santana, you can sleep in a traditional A-shaped cottage. *Hortensia Gardens: Quinta Gorick, Caminho dos Pretos 89, São João Latrão. Map H5. 291 795 219. € • Residencial Prisma: Água de Pena, Machico; Map K4; 291 524 185; € • O Escondidinho das Canas: Pico António Fernandes, Santana; Map H2; 291 572 319; €*

10 Rural Tourism

Madeira Rural is an online booking agent for 20 or so properties around the island, from converted farm buildings to cottages. *www.madeirarural.com*

General Index

Phrase Book

In an Emergency

Help!	**Socorro!**	soo-**koh**-roo
Stop!	**Páre!**	**pahr'**
Call a! doctor!	**Chame um médico!**	**shahm'** ooñ **meh**-dee-koo
Call an ambulance!	**Chame uma ambulância!**	**shahm'** oo-muh **añ**-boo-**lañ**-see-uh
Call the police!	**Chame a polícia!**	**shahm'** uh poo-**lee**-see-uh
Call the fire brigade!	**Chame os bombeiros!**	**shahm'** oosh bom-**bay**-roosh
Where is the nearest telephone?	**Há um telefone aqui perto?**	**ah** ooñ te-le-**fon'** uh-**kee pehr**-too
Where is the nearest hospital?	**Onde é o hospital mais próximo?**	ond' **eh** oo **ohsh**-pee-**tahl' mysh pro**-see-moo

Communication Essentials

Yes	**Sim**	**seeñ**
No	**Não**	**nowñ**
Please	**Por favor/ Faz favor**	poor fuh-**vor fash** fuh-**vor**
Thank you	**Obrigado/da**	o-bree-**gah**-doo/duh
Excuse me	**Desculpe**	dish-**koolp'**
Hello	**Olá**	oh-**lah**
Goodbye	**Adeus**	a-**deh**-oosh
Good morning	**Bom-dia**	boñ **dee**-uh
Good afternoon	**Boa-tarde**	**boh**-uh **tard'**
Good night	**Boa-noite**	**boh**-uh **noyt'**
Yesterday	**Ontem**	oñ-**tayñ**
Today	**Hoje**	**ohj'**
Tomorrow	**Amanhã**	**ah**-man **yañ**
Here	**Aqui**	uh-**kee**
There	**Ali**	uh-**lee**
What?	**O quê?**	**oo** keh
Which?	**Qual?**	**kwahl'**
When?	**Quando?**	**kwañ**-doo
Why?	**Porquê?**	**poor**-keh
Where?	**Onde?**	**oñd'**

Useful Phrases

How are you?	**Como está?**	**koh**-moo **shtah**
Very well, thank you.	**Bem, obrigado/da.**	**bayñ** o-bree **gah**-doo/duh
Pleased to meet you	**Encantado/da.**	eñ-kañ-**tah**-doo/duh
See you soon.	**Até logo.**	uh-**teh loh**-goo
That's fine.	**Está bem.**	**shtah bayñ**
Where is/are…?	**Onde está/ estão…?**	**ond' shtah/ shtowñ**
How far is it to…?	**A que distância fica…?**	uh kee dish-**tañ**-see-uh **fee**-kuh
Which way to…?	**Como se vai para…?**	**koh**-moo seh **vy** puh-ruh
Do you speak English?	**Fala Inglês?**	**fah**-luh eeñ-**glehsh**
I don't understand.	**Não compreendo.**	nowñ kom-pree-**en**-doo
I'm sorry.	**Desculpe.**	dish-**koolp'**
Could you speak more slowly please?	**Pode falar mais devagar por favor?**	**pohd'** fuh-**lar mysh** d'-va-**gar** poor fah-**vor**

Sightseeing

cathedral	**sé**	**seh**
church	**igreja**	ee-**gray**-juh
garden	**jardim**	jar-**deeñ**
library	**biblioteca**	bee-blee-oo-**teh**-kuh
museum	**museu**	moo-**zeh**-oo
tourist information	**posto de turismo**	**posh**-too d' too-**reesh**-moo
closed for holidays	**fechado para férias**	fe-**sha**-doo puh-ruh **feh**-ree-ash
bus station	**estação de autocarros**	shta-sowñ d' oh-too-**kah**-roosh
railway station	**estação de comboios**	shta-**sowñ** d' koñ-**boy**-oosh
azulejo	uh-zoo-**lay**-joo	painted ceramic tile
Manuelino	ma-noo-el-**ee**-noo	Manueline (late Gothic architectural style)

Useful Words

big	**grande**	**grand'**
small	**pequeno**	pe-**keh**-noo
hot	**quente**	**kent'**
cold	**frio**	**free**-oo
good	**bom**	**boñ**
bad	**mau**	**mah**-oo
enough	**bastante**	bash-**tant'**
well	**bem**	**bayñ**
open	**aberto**	a-**behr**-too
closed	**fechado**	fe-**shah**-doo
left	**esquerda**	**shkehr**-duh
right	**direita**	dee-**ray**-tuh
straight on	**em frente**	ayñ **frent'**
near	**perto**	**pehr**-too
far	**longe**	**loñj'**
up	**suba**	**soo**-bah
down	**desça**	**deh**-shuh
early	**cedo**	**seh**-doo
late	**tarde**	**tard'**
entrance	**entrada**	en-**trah**-duh
exit	**saída**	sa-**ee**-duh
toilets	**casa de banho**	**kah**-zuh d' **ban**-yoo
more	**mais**	**mysh**
less	**menos**	**meh**-noosh

Shopping

How much does this cost?	**Quanto custa isto?**	**kwan**-too **koosh**-tuh **eesh**-too
I would like …	**Queria …**	**kree**-uh
I'm just looking.	**Estou só a ver obrigado/a.**	**shtoh soh** uh **vehr** o-bree-**gah**-doo/uh
Do you take credit cards?	**Aceita cartões de crédito?**	uh-**say**-tuh kar-**toinsh** de **kreh**-dee-too?
What time do you open?	**A que horas abre?**	uh **kee oh**-rash **ah**-bre?
What time do you close?	**A que horas fecha?**	uh **kee oh**-rash **fay**-shuh?
this one	**este**	**ehst'**
that one	**esse**	**ehss'**
expensive	**caro**	**kah**-roo

cheap	**barato**	buh-**rah**-too
size (clothes/ shoes)	**número**	**noom'**-roo
white	**branco**	**brañ**-koo
black	**preto**	**preh**-too
red	**roxo**	**roh**-shoo
yellow	**amarelo**	uh-muh-**reh**-loo
green	**verde**	**vehrd'**
blue	**azul**	uh-**zool'**

Types of Shop

antique shop	**loja de antiguidades**	**loh**-juh de an-tee-gwee-**dahd'sh**
bakery	**padaria**	**pah**-duh-**ree**-uh
bank	**banco**	**bañ**-koo
bookshop	**livraria**	lee-vruh-**ree**-uh
butcher	**talho**	**tah**-lyoo
cake shop	**pastelaria**	pash-te-luh-**ree**-uh
chemist	**farmácia**	far-**mah**-see-uh
fishmonger	**peixaria**	pay-shuh-**ree**-uh
hair dresser	**cabelereiro**	kab'-lay-**ray**-roo
market	**mercado**	mehr-**kah**-doo
newsagent	**kiosque**	kee-**yohsk'**
post office	**correios**	koo-**ray**-oosh
shoe shop	**sapataria**	suh-puh-tuh-**ree**-uh
supermarket	**supermercado**	**soo**-pehr-mer-**kah**-doo
tobacconist	**tabacaria**	tuh-buh-kuh-**ree**-uh
travel agency	**agência de viagens**	uh-jeñ-**see**-uh de vee-**ah**-jayñsh

Staying in a Hotel

Do you have a vacant room?	**Tem um quarto livre?**	**tayñ** ooñ **kwar**-too **leevr'**
room with a bath	**um quarto com casa de banho**	ooñ **kwar**-too koñ **kah**-zuh d' ban-**yoo**
shower	**duche**	**doosh**
single room	**quarto individual**	**kwar**-too een-dee-vee-doo-**ahl'**
double room	**quarto de casal**	**kwar**-too d' kuh-**zhal'**
twin room	**quarto com duas camas**	**kwar**-too koñ **doo**-ash **kah**-mash
porter	**porteiro**	poor-**tay**-roo
key	**chave**	**shahv'**
I have a reservation.	**Tenho um quarto reservado.**	**tayn**-yoo ooñ **kwar**-too re-ser-**vah**-doo

Eating Out

Have you got a table for …?	**Tem uma mesa para … ?**	**tayñ** oo-muh **meh**-zuh puh-ruh
I am a vegetarian.	**Sou vegetariano/a.**	Soh ve-je-tuh-ree-**ah**-noo/uh
Waiter!	**Por favor!/ Faz favor!**	poor fuh-**vor** **fash** fuh-**vor**
I'd like to reserve a table.	**Quero reservar una mesa.**	**keh**-roo re-zehr-**var** oo-muh **meh**-zuh
The bill, please.	**A conta por favor/faz favor.**	uh **kohn**-tuh poor fuh-**vor**/ **fash** fuh-**vor**
the menu	**a lista**	uh **leesh**-tuh
fixed-price menu	**a ementa turística**	uh ee-**mehn**-tuh too-**reesh**-tee-kuh
wine list	**a lista de vinhos**	uh **leesh**-tuh de **veen**-yoosh
glass	**um copo**	ooñ **koh**-poo
bottle	**uma garrafa**	oo-muh guh-**rah**-fuh
half bottle	**meia-garrafa**	**may**-uh guh-**rah**-fuh
knife	**uma faca**	oo-mah **fah**-kuh
fork	**um garfo**	ooñ **gar**-foo
spoon	**uma colher**	oo-muh kool-**yair**
plate	**um prato**	ooñ **prah**-too
breakfast	**pequeno-almoço**	pe-**keh**-noo-ahl-**moh**-soo
lunch	**almoço**	ahl-**moh**-soo
dinner	**jantar**	jan-**tar**
cover	**couvert**	koo-**vehr**
starter	**entrada**	en-**trah**-duh
main course	**prato principal**	**prah**-too prin-see-**pahl'**
dish of the day	**prato do dia**	**prah**-too doo **dee**-uh
set dish	**combinado**	koñ-bee-**nah**-doo
half portion	**meia-dose**	may-uh **doh**-se
dessert	**sobremesa**	**soh**-bre-**meh**-zuh
rare	**mal passado**	**mahl'** puh-**sah**-doo
medium	**médio**	**meh**-dee-oo
well done	**bem passado**	**bayñ** puh-**sah**-doo

Menu Decoder

abacate	uh-buh-**kaht'**	avocado
açorda	uh-**sor**-duh	bread- and garlic-based soup
açúcar	uh-**soo**-kuhr	sugar
água mineral	**ah**-gwuh mee-ne-**rahl'**	mineral water
alho	**ahl**-yoo	garlic
alperce	ahl'-**pehrce**	apricot
amêijoas	uh-**may**-joo-ush	clams
ananás	uh-nuh-**nahsh**	pineapple
anona	ah-**noh**-nah	custard apple
arroz	uh-**rohsh**	rice
assado	uh-**sah**-doo	baked
atum	uh-**tooñ**	tuna
aves	**ah**-vesh	poultry
azeite	uh-**zayt'**	olive oil
azeitonas	uh-zay-**toh**-nash	olives
bacalhau	buh-kuh-**lyow**	dried, salted cod
banana	buh-**nah**-nuh	banana
batatas	buh-**tah**-tash	potatoes
batatas fritas	buh-**tah**-tash **free**-tash	french fries
batido	buh-**tee**-doo	milk-shake
bica	**bee**-kuh	espresso
bife	**beef**	steak
bolacha	boo-**lah**-shuh	biscuit
bolo	**boh**-loo	cake
bolo de caco	**boh**-loo d' **kah**-koh	Madeiran bread

caça	**kah**-ssuh	game
café	kuh-**feh**	coffee
camarões	kuh-muh-**roysh**	large prawns
carangueijo	kuh-rañ **gay**-yoo	crab
carne	**karn'**	meat
castanhas	cash-**tahn**-yush	chestnuts
cebola	se-**boh**-luh	onion
cerejas	sehr-**ray**-jahs	cherries
cerveja	sehr-**vay**-juh	beer
chá	**shah**	tea
cherne	**shern'**	stone bass
chocolate	shoh-koh-**laht'**	chocolate
chocos	**shoh**-koosh	cuttlefish
chouriço	shoh-**ree**-soo	red, spicy sausage
churrasco	shoo-**rash**-coo	on the spit
coelho	koo-**el**-yoo	rabbit
cogumelos	koo-goo-**meh**-loosh	mushrooms
cordeiro	kur-**deh**-roo	lamb
cozido	koo-**zee**-doo	boiled
dourada	doh-**rah**-dah	sea bream
espada	(e)sh-**pah**-dah	scabbard fish
espetada	(e)sh-puh-**tah**-dah	Madeiran beef kebab
espadarte	(e)sh-pah-**dahr**-tuh	swordfish
fiambre	fee-**ambri**	ham
frango	**fran**-goo	chicken
frito	**free**-too	fried
fruta	**froo**-tuh	fruit
gambas	**gam**-bash	prawns
gelado	je-**lah**-doo	ice cream
gelo	**jeh**-loo	ice
goiaba	goy-**ah**-bah	guava
grelhado	grel-**yah**-doo	grilled
kiwi	**kee**-wee	kiwi fruit
lagosta	luh-**gohsh**-tuh	lobster
lapas	**lah**-push	limpets
laranja	luh **rañ**-juh	orange
leite	**layt'**	milk
limão	lee-**mowñ**	lemon
limonada	lee-moo-**nah**-duh	lemonade
linguado	leeñ-**gwah**-doo	sole
lulas	**loo**-lash	squid
maçã	muh-**sañ**	apple
manga	**mahn**-gah	mango
manteiga	mañ-**tay**-guh	butter
maracujá	muhr-ah-koo-**jah**	passion fruit
mariscos	muh-**reesh**-koosh	seafood
milho frito	**meel**-yoo **free**-too	deep-fried cubes of maize meal
morangos	moh-**rahn**-gosh	strawberries
ostras	**osh**-trash	oysters
ovos	**oh**-voosh	eggs
pão	**powñ**	bread
pargo	**pahr**-goo	red bream
pastel	pash-**tehl'**	cake
peixe	**paysh'**	fish
pêssego	**pess**-eh-goo	peach
pêssego careca	**pess**-eh-goo kah-**ray**-kuh	nectarine
pimenta	pee-**men**-tuh	pepper
polvo	**pohl'**-voo	octopus
porco	**por**-coo	pork
prego	**pray**-goh	steak sandwich
queijo	**kay**-joo	cheese
sal	**sahl'**	salt
salada	suh-**lah**-duh	salad
salsichas	sahl-**see**-shash	sausages
sandes	**san**-desh	sandwich
sopa	**soh**-puh	soup
sumo	**soo**-moo	juice
tamboril	tam-boo-**ril'**	monkfish
tarte	**tart'**	pie/cake
tamarilho	tahm-ah-**reel**-yoo	tomarillo
tomate	too-**maht'**	tomato
torrada	too-**rah**-duh	toast
tosta	**tohsh**-tuh	toasted sandwich
vinagre	vee-**nah**-gre	vinegar
vinho branco	**veen**-yoo **brañ**-koo	white wine
vinho tinto	**veen**-yoo **teen**-too	red wine
vitela	vee-**teh**-luh	veal

Numbers

0	**zero**	**zeh**-roo
1	**um**	**ooñ**
2	**dois**	**doysh**
3	**três**	**tresh**
4	**quatro**	**kwa**-troo
5	**cinco**	**seeñ**-koo
6	**seis**	**saysh**
7	**sete**	**set'**
8	**oito**	**oy**-too
9	**nove**	**nov'**
10	**dez**	de-**esh**
11	**onze**	**oñz'**
12	**doze**	**doz'**
13	**treze**	**trez'**
14	**catorze**	ka-**torz'**
15	**quinze**	**keeñz'**
16	**dezasseis**	de-zuh-**saysh**
17	**dezassete**	de-zuh-**set'**
18	**dezoito**	de-**zoy**-too
19	**dezanove**	de-zuh-**nov'**
20	**vinte**	**veent'**
21	**vinte e um**	**veen**-**tee**-ooñ
30	**trinta**	**treeñ**-tuh
40	**quarenta**	kwa-**ren**-tuh
50	**cinquenta**	seen-**kwen**-tuh
60	**sessenta**	se-**sen**-tuh
70	**setenta**	se-**ten**-tuh
80	**oitenta**	oy-**ten**-tuh
90	**noventa**	noo-**ven**-tuh
100	**cem**	**sayñ**
101	**cento e um**	**sen**-too-ee-ooñ
102	**cento e dois**	**sen**-too-ee-**doysh**
200	**duzentos**	doo-**zen**-toosh
300	**trezentos**	tre-**zen**-toosh
400	**quatrocentos**	**kwa**-troo-**sen**-toosh
500	**quinhentos**	kee-**nyen**-toosh
600	**seiscentos**	saysh-**sen**-toosh
700	**setecentos**	set'-**sen**-toosh
800	**oitocentos**	**oy**-too-**sen**-toosh
900	**novecentos**	nov'-**sen**-toosh
1,000	**mil**	**meel'**

Time

one minute	**um minuto**	ooñ mee-**noo**-too
one hour	**uma hora**	**oo**-muh **oh**-ruh
half an hour	**meia-hora**	**may**-uh **oh**-ruh
Monday	**segunda-feira**	se-**goon**-duh-**fay**-ruh
Tuesday	**terça-feira**	**ter**-sa-**fay**-ruh
Wednesday	**quarta-feira**	**kwar**-ta-**fay**-ruh
Thursday	**quinta-feira**	**keen**-ta-**fay**-ruh
Friday	**sexta-feira**	**say**-shta-**fay**-ruh
Saturday	**sábado**	**sah**-ba-too

Acknowledgments

The Author

Christopher Catling has written more than 50 travel guides, including best-selling DK *Eyewitness* guides to Florence and Venice. He also contributed to the Portugal, Italy and Great Britain guides in the same series. When not writing books, he works as an archaeologist and heritage consultant. He is a Fellow of the Society of Antiquaries and the Royal Society of Arts, and a member of the British Guild of Travel Writers. He loves Madeira, and never grows tired of visiting it to walk, and to enjoy the food and warm hospitality of the islanders.

Special thanks for their invaluable assistance to Dorita Mendonça at the Madeira Tourist Board in Funchal, Marta Henriques at the Madeira Promotion Bureau and Elsa Cortez at the Portuguese National Tourist Office in London.

Produced by DP Services, a division of DUNCAN PETERSEN PUBLISHING LTD, 31 Ceylon Road, London W14 0PY

Project Editor Chris Barstow
Designer Ian Midson
Picture Researcher Lily Sellar
Listings Researcher Tomas Tranæus
Indexer Hilary Bird
Proofreader Yoko Kawaguchi
Main Photographer Antony Souter
Additional Photography Paul Bernhardt, Linda Whitwam, Rough Guides/Matthew Hancock, Rough Guides/Helena Smith
Illustrator Chapel Design & Marketing
Maps John Plumer, JP Map Graphics

Cartography Credits

Madeira base map derived from Madeira Tourist Board, www.madeiratourism.org

For Dorling Kindersley
Publisher Douglas Amrine
Senior Art Editor Tessa Bindloss
Senior Cartographic Editor Casper Morris
Senior DTP Designer Jason Little
Production Linda Dare
Picture Librarian Romaine Werblow

Revisions Team Namrata Adhwaryu, Emma Anacootee, Paul Bernhardt, Marta Bescos, Sophie Black, Claire Jones, Cincy Jose, Juliet Kenny, Priya Kukadia, Carly Madden, Alison McGill, Jane Oliver-Jedrzejak, Jude Ledger, Darren Longley, Tanya Mahendru, Nicola Malone, Sangita Patel, Mary Ormandy, Maria Luísa Perestrello, Marianne Petrou, Mani Ramaswamy, Lucy Richards, Sumita Khatwani, Tomas Tranæus, Dora Whitaker, Kaberi Hazarika, Khushboo Priya, Ajay Verma.

Picture Credits

Placement Key: a-above; b-below/bottom; c-centre; f-far; l-left; r-right; t-top.

The publishers would like to thank the following individuals, companies and picture libraries for permission to reproduce their photographs:

ALAMY: Eric James 102 tl; LOOK Die Bildagentur der Fotografen GmbH 30cl; Robert Harding Picture Library 32–33c; BELMOND REID'S PALACE: 36tl; E PRA PICANHA: 72TL; FUNCHAL DESIGN HOTEL: 114TR; Ernst Wrba 29b; LEONARDO MEDIA LTD.: 112tr; MARTIN SIEPMANN: 23b, 33cra; MARY EVANS PICTURE LIBRARY: 37tr, 37bl; MICHELLE CHAPLOW: 61tr, 61br; MUSEU DE ARTE SACRA DO FUNCHAL: 10b; NATIONAL MARITIME MUSEUM, LONDON: 36c; PESTANA HOTELS AND RESORTS: 99tl; POWERSTOCK: 54cl; PRISMA: 92–93; ; TERRAS DE AVENTURA: 48cl; TOPFOTO: 37cr, 37br, TURISMO DA MADEIRA: 19tl, 26cl, 30b, 54tl, 54tr, 55bl, 55cr.

For jacket credits see Contents page. All other images are © Dorling Kindersley. For further information see www.dkimages.com

Selected Index of Places